SHINING MOMENTS

VOLUME 2

SHINING MOMENTS

VOLUME 2

STORIES FOR LATTER-DAY SAINT CHILDREN

BY LUCILE C. READING

Deseret Book ®

Salt Lake City, Utah

No part of this book may be reproduced in any
form or by any means without permission in writing
from the publisher, Deseret Book Company,
P.O. Box 30178, Salt Lake City, Utah 84130.
Deseret Book is a registered trademark of
Deseret Book Company.

First printing May 1986
Second printing November 1987
Third printing February 1989

Library of Congress Cataloging-in-Publication Data
(Revised for volume 2)

Reading, Lucile C.
    Shining moments.

    Includes index.
    A collection of true stories reflecting Mormon values.
        1. Children—Religious life.   2. Christian life—
Mormon authors—Juvenile literature.   3. Mormons.
4. Christian life.   I. Title.
BX8656.R4   1985   242'.62   85-1655
ISBN 0-87747-687-X (v. 1)
ISBN 0-87579-044-5 (v. 2)

CONTENTS

PUBLISHER'S PREFACE

"Shining Moments" was a popular series in the *Children's Friend* and the *Friend* magazines until the death of its author, Lucile Cardon Reading, on March 22, 1983. That series provided the material for the books *Shining Moments* and *Shining Moments, Volume 2*.

Most of the stories in the first volume came from material submitted to the magazines by members of The Church of Jesus Christ of Latter-day Saints about their own children or children they knew. Sister Reading took these true incidents and wrote them as stories for the series.

Most of the stories in the second volume came from material Sister Reading found in reputable magazines, newspapers, and books. She was especially careful to document the sources she used and to use material about incidents that actually happened. Above all, she sought for stories about people who would inspire greater faith and courage in the lives of Latter-day Saint children.

SHINING MOMENTS
IN THE LIVES
OF CHILDREN
PAST AND PRESENT

RESCUE

It had been a long, hot, and especially dry summer. Then one Monday morning in early September it began to rain. At first there was only a drizzle of moisture, but late in the afternoon the storm became periodically violent as flashes of lightning chased across the sullen sky.

As twelve-year-old Krista and her sister prepared dinner, they often stopped at the window and anxiously peered through the rain. They didn't mind the storm—their concern was for Father and the word he would bring about Mother and their baby brother, whom their parents had taken hundreds of miles away to a hospital for surgery.

Everything was ready when Father finally arrived home. Before eating, however, he suggested that they all kneel down for family prayer. They prayed for help for their baby and then asked for a special blessing that Father and the three girls left at home might be protected from harm while Mother was away.

Rain poured down all during dinner. Just as they agreed that it was a good night to be at home, the phone rang. Father was a dentist, and the caller was a patient who needed emergency treatment for an aching tooth. Krista asked if she might ride to the office with Father. Together they splashed through the rain, jumped into the car, and headed for the dental office. They gave little thought to men sandbagging areas that had been flooded some years ago after a heavy storm.

It was still storming when in pitchy blackness they left the office and started for home. All went well until Father made a sharp turn off the freeway. Just as he did, someone on a high bank opposite frantically honked a horn to warn him away, but the warning came too late! Rushing floodwaters engulfed the car, lifting and twisting it. Father managed to push Krista partway through a window so two boys on the bank could pull her out and carry her to safety, but it was impossible for him to climb out of the car himself. As the car was swept along on the crest of the flood, he was torn out of it and sucked into a long drain tunnel. The last sound he heard before he went under was Krista screaming, "Daddy, Daddy!" as she struggled to get away from those who held her tight to prevent her from jumping into the raging stream after her father.

Gasping for air, he was washed through the drain. Strong arms lifted him from the whirling water at the end of the tunnel. After several long moments of frantic suspense, Krista and her father were together again—cut and bruised but somehow miraculously alive.

As Krista's father held her tight, they both managed a feeble smile. Safe in her father's arms, Krista breathed with relief as they looked deep into each other's eyes.

"We had a quick answer to our family prayer, didn't we, darling?" Father said.

Krista looked up at him and smiled. She couldn't find the words to express her feeling of love and gratitude, so she just nodded in full agreement.

JERRY'S DREAM

"Next Saturday you're invited to go to Mont du Lac and see the skiers," Mother told Jerry one snowy morning in January. He could hardly believe the good news.

For months, while other boys and girls were playing in the deep Minnesota snow, he had watched them from his chair at the window. Not being able to swim and play baseball in the summer didn't trouble Jerry as much as being handicapped in the winter. In winter the snow looked so inviting, and children of almost every age were outside making snowmen, playing Fox and Geese, or pulling sleds up the hill so they could slide back down.

But more than anything else, Jerry longed to be able to ski. Even before polio struck its crippling blow, he had eagerly listened to stories from those who went to nearby Mont du Lac each winter. He had secretly planned to be a skier himself when he became a little older and had earned enough money to buy skis.

After his illness he had almost given up the dream of ever going down the steep slopes himself, but he still clung to the hope that some time he could go to Mont du Lac and at least watch others ski. Now he was actually able to go there!

It seemed as if Saturday would never come, but finally it did. Early that morning the big special bus pulled up to the little house where Jerry lived. What an air of excitement there was as he, with other crippled boys and girls, watched the beautiful white world outside as the bus traveled through the pines almost to the top of the mountain.

At the ski center, chairs had been arranged on a special platform so the children could be carried or pushed close to the end of the ski runs. Even though the cold made his legs ache, Jerry thought it was wonderful to be at Mont du Lac.

But how much more wonderful it would be, he thought wistfully, if only he could know the feeling of flying down the snowy slopes! Almost without realizing it, he sighed and said aloud to himself, "Oh, how I wish I could ski down that slope even once."

The next thing he knew, strong arms lifted him up, and he heard the ski master say, "Well, if you want it that much, you can do it—and right now!"

The man jabbed his ski poles into the snow, cradled Jerry tightly in his arms, glided over to the ski tow, grasped the rope with his left hand, and up they went—up and up to the very top of the run.

The man looked down at the happy boy and asked if he were comfortable and ready. Still too surprised to speak, Jerry nodded.

It almost took his breath away when the ski master flew down the first dizzy drop of the headwall. Then out into the open slopes they skimmed in great sweeping curves, snow billowing up like clouds behind them. Finally they skidded to a stop near the other children.

As Jerry watched, the ski master carried some of

the other boys and girls up the tow and then swept down the slope with them.

Jerry forgot the cold. He even forgot his crippled legs. For at least a moment it seemed that his dream of becoming a skier had really come true.

NEW SHOES!

The boys and girls of Drancy school, the very poorest in all of Paris, were breathless with excitement. The long-awaited day had come at last—the day on which the children would receive 300 pairs of brand new shoes sent through the American Red Cross.

The day was cold and foggy, but inside the little schoolhouse it was warm and bright. The shoes were set on long tables, and inside each one was a rare treat, a chocolate bar. A flower had been placed on top of each pair of shoes. The children had gathered the flowers to celebrate this exciting day, for it had been years since any of them had owned a pair of brand-new leather shoes.

On every foot was an old wooden shoe or a ragged sandal with cloth soles. All were poorly fit, some handed down from grown-ups who could no longer use the shoes.

The boys and girls stood quietly around the long tables. No one touched the shoes. No one spoke. Not even a whisper was heard until the teacher signaled for the children to sing. They had learned "The Star-Spangled Banner" for the wonderful occasion. Then the boys and girls sang the national anthem in French.

Every eye was shining, and every heart was beating with excitement—but not one hand stretched out to touch a shoe. The children just looked and looked.

Finally they ran out into the schoolyard to play. Some of the girls stopped to print thank-you notes on scraps of paper to be sent to the givers, but no one picked up a single shoe to even try it on.

The officials who had delivered the shoes did not understand this. Then the teacher explained, "Tomorrow the children will try on the shoes. Today they have seen them. That is enough. They are happy. Do you know what a wonderful thing it can be just to expect new shoes?"

THE CHRISTMAS LETTER

It was almost Christmas, but there was no feeling of joy in Marian's home. She remembered other Christmases when there had been—when Daddy would come home from his work in the dead-letter section of the post office with a happy smile on his face as he greeted her, her little brother, and Mummie. What jokes and fun and pleasant talk there had been then, with stories before bedtime.

All of this was before her little brother had suddenly become sick and then quickly died before anyone could help him. It seemed to Marian that, in a way, her daddy had died too, because he never smiled anymore nor told her stories nor greeted her with a hug and kiss. In fact, he didn't seem to care whether she and Mummie were even around.

Marian couldn't talk to Mummie about the problem, for that would only make her sadder. She didn't think anyone else could understand how it had been in their home and how it was now.

Then one day the idea of writing a letter came to her. It wasn't easy to write such an important letter all by herself. But when it was finished, Marian addressed it to the North Pole and posted it in the corner mailbox. The letter said:

Dear Santa Claus:
    We are sad at our house. My little brother went to heaven last spring. . . You needn't mind leaving me anything, but if you could give Daddy something that would make him like he used to be, I do wish you would. I heard him say to Mummie that only Eternity could cure him. Could you bring him some of that?
                    Marian

It was more than a coincidence that the letter reached the dead-letter desk of Marian's father instead of being checked by some other man in the department.

Later that day when Daddy came home, it was almost as if Christmas had come already, for as he opened the door, there was a wide smile on his face. He paused for just a moment, then opened his arms wide, just as he used to do, and took both Mummie and Marian into them. The concern of a young daughter had indeed brought back a bit of eternal love to her family.

AN HONEST ANSWER

There lived in Connecticut a girl named Hetty Marvin. Her cousin was governor. At one time he had to flee for his life and hide from his enemies in the Marvin home.

The next morning Hetty was sent to bleach some cloth in a nearby meadow. She was told to turn it in the sun from one side to the other. As she started to do so, the governor came running down the path. He stopped to ask Hetty to tell the soldiers, who had come to search for him, that he had gone down the road.

"Then," said the governor, "I'll go in the opposite direction down to the river, and they won't be able to catch me."

"I can't do that," answered Hetty, "for I'd be telling a lie."

"But you must help me," he begged, "or I may lose my life."

"Hide under this pile of linen," Hetty said, "and I won't tell anyone where you are even if I'm killed for it."

The sound of horses coming toward them could be

heard in the distance. "It's my only chance," he said. "I'll get down as you say."

The young girl covered him completely just as some soldiers on horseback rode up to her.

"Did you see a man running by here?" asked the captain.

Hetty nodded.

"Which way did he go, child?"

"I promised not to tell, sir," said Hetty quietly.

"But you must," said the captain, "or you'll be punished."

Hetty refused to answer even though others in the group tried to get her to do so. Finally one of the men said, "If you won't tell us which way the governor went, then just tell us the last thing he said to you."

"His last words were, 'It's my only chance. I'll get down as you say.'"

The men nodded in silent agreement and then turned their horses toward the river, thinking the words meant that the governor would get down to the river.

FOR A BRAVE GIRL

Show and Tell Time is usually exciting as boys and girls share their experiences and their treasures with others. But this morning something special was felt by each one in the kindergarten room as five-year-old Margaret told again what had happened when she had gone home for lunch the day before.

As she had skipped toward the house where she lived, her thoughts were of her twenty-month-old brother, David, who had been left in the care of a babysitter while their mother worked. Margaret hoped he would still be awake so he could sit in his high chair and talk with her as she ate lunch. Afterwards, he could play with her before his afternoon nap.

When Margaret stepped into the kitchen, there was a strange smell. An even stranger sight greeted her. Over in the corner, smoke was curling up behind the clothes dryer, and then flames suddenly leaped up the wall.

David was nowhere to be seen. In a flash Margaret realized that he must already be upstairs with the babysitter for his nap and that both of them would be unaware of the smoke and flames below. She ran to the stairs shouting, "Fire! Fire!"

The babysitter raced down the stairs with David while Margaret ran next door to a neighbor to get help and to call the fire department. This neighbor later described her as "very calm—a real little soldier."

When a newspaper reporter interviewed her and asked, "Weren't you afraid?" Margaret explained, "No, I wasn't. It was my brother I really was scared about, and that's who I prayed for."

A breathless hush fell over the schoolroom as Margaret concluded her story. The children in her class looked at her in amazement. Then each one cheered with approval when their teacher gave Margaret a bright and shiny badge on which were inscribed these words: "For a Brave Girl."

This was a happy moment for Margaret, but the happiest one of all had been after the fire when David put his arms around her neck and hugged her especially tight.

THE BOY WRANGLER

Every cowboy of the Big Bar Cross Cattle Company watched Gene as he came out of the bunkhouse and walked across the yard to the corral. He was only thirteen and small for his age. He thought there was something strange about the way the men were all on hand watching him, and he felt uneasy in his ragged clothes. Often in the past few months they had scolded him about them, and sometimes their language as they did so had made the boy squirm.

Gene especially remembered a wet cold day a few weeks previous. The men tried to send him back to the bunkhouse for a warm jacket or a rain slicker, and they looked at him with disbelief when he only shrugged his shoulders and mumbled, "Haven't got one." That night several of them tried to talk to him about why he was using his saddle blanket for a bed roll. They had been full of questions, and the boy had been worrying ever since. One day he overheard one say something about the "raggedy little rascal," and another suggested that Gene "didn't have enough sense to fear a bad man or a bad horse."

Gene knew these men weren't bad—only tough and rough—but he wondered as he walked toward

17

them what they might have in mind as they carefully eyed him. They couldn't know, Gene thought, how desperately he needed the job so he could send money home to his widowed mother, and he supposed they'd laugh at him if they ever knew how much he cared about being accepted by the men.

He remembered how hurt he had been when one of them had taunted him by saying, "You're just too miserly to get rigged out decent." He had never let them know how he longed and prayed for a day when he could have good clothes and a real saddle instead of the one he had gotten in exchange for soap coupons he had saved.

Suddenly the ranch foreman stepped forward, and then the rest of the cowboys closed in around the boy. From the back of the circle, a big box was handed from man to man and put into Gene's hands. No one said a word as the boy awkwardly held it and looked from one to the other, his heart heavy with worry and fear. He wondered what trick they had planned.

Then came a shout from one of the men, "Open it!" It was soon picked up and echoed from all, "Open it! Open it!"

They somehow had found out that the boy was sending all his money home. Each man had made a contribution to order a complete cowboy outfit. Gene carefully opened the box, looked at the outfit, and then looked up at the men, his eyes shining through misty tears.

The men had often said to each other, "That kid is gritty," and they prided themselves on their own toughness. But as they watched Gene they sensed the depth of his surprise and joy, and their own eyes were wet as their gaze met that of the boy wrangler in full acceptance—and with love.

THE JUMPING ROPE

It had always seemed a long way to LuAnn to ride from her home in Oregon to the Primary Children's Hospital in Salt Lake City, Utah. She had made the trip many times.

This time the miles went by more slowly than ever. Today the doctor would tell her if she could do what other children could do. Most of all, she hoped he would tell her that she could use her jump rope.

The trees had worn brilliant fall colors the last time the Nelsons had taken LuAnn to Salt Lake. Mother had said then that the world looked so cheerful she just knew good news awaited them. And, sure enough, the doctor had agreed to let LuAnn go to school each day. "Come back after the holidays," he'd said, "and we'll see how your heart likes school."

The holidays were over. Snow covered the ground. The sky was a heavy gray, and Mother sighed quietly once and then sighed again. Even Father had nothing to say.

Finally Mother broke the silence. "How do you feel, LuAnn?" she asked. "Getting tired?"

"I'm not tired," LuAnn answered. "I'm just anxious to get out my jump rope. Everything's going to be just fine."

She smiled. Her face shone as it had that morning months before when the nurse had wheeled her down the hall to the doctor who was to perform heart surgery. LuAnn had looked up at her father and mother. She had smiled at them then too and said, "Everything's going to be just fine. I've asked Heavenly Father to bless me and the doctors."

That January afternoon at the Primary Children's Hospital the doctor straightened up after a careful examination of LuAnn. "You had better stop on your way back to Oregon," he told LuAnn's father, "and pick up a brand new rope for a little girl whose heart really seems to like going to school!"

THE STRANGE WHISTLE

The boys and girls were dressed in their Sunday best. Some carried flowers, and others carried flags to celebrate the exciting event. Long before noon they and many adults had assembled on top of high bluffs and buildings to watch for the tracklayers of the Union Pacific Railroad, who were due to arrive in Ogden, Utah, that day, Monday, March 8, 1869.

It was almost noon when happy shouts announced that the tracklayers were in sight, putting down the rails as fast as they could, followed close behind by a steam locomotive. By 2:30 in the afternoon, when the train actually came into the city, flags were flying, brass bands were playing, and its long-awaited arrival was greeted with wild enthusiasm.

Eight-year-old Dianna and her friends, carrying flowers and flags, edged as close to the track as they dared. As the last rail into Ogden was laid, the engineer brought the big steam engine to a halt, its whistle shrilly shrieking above the noise of the crowd.

At the strange, never-heard-before sound, Dianna threw down her flowers, picked up the hem of her ankle-length dress, and ran as fast as she could

21

away from the scene, her friends running close behind her. They stopped only when swampy ground a half mile away mired them down almost to their waists. Still they could hear in the distance the weird whistle blowing and blowing.

Many years later, after those boys and girls had become used to trains, they would recall with a laugh the first time they had seen the "fiery steed" and heard the frightening sound it had made.

A DOG'S BEST FRIEND

A boy sat on a New York subway one day holding in his arms a sickly looking Boston terrier. The dog had been hurt. Clumsy bandages tied around its leg showed that the boy had tried to doctor his pet. It was hard to tell which was the more pitiful sight—the boy or the dog.

Across from them sat a big rough-looking truck driver. He couldn't help looking at the boy and the dog and wishing he could think of something to do. Finally he turned to the man sitting next to him and asked, "Did you ever see such a sorry sight in your life?"

The man shook his head in understanding.

The little dog whined in pain, and the boy hugged the animal closer to him while a solitary tear slid down his cheek. This was too much for the truck driver. He leaned across the aisle. "What's the matter, sonny?" he questioned.

"My dog's been hurt," the boy answered. "Pop says I have to take him to the humane society because we haven't any money for a vet. And you know what I've heard? If he's hurt too bad, they'll gas him. Boy, have I been praying that he'll be all right!"

The truck driver looked again at the dog and then at the people in the subway car. Finally he stood up. "Folks," he called in a loud voice. The noise in the car stopped. The truck driver went on, "This boy has trouble. We're spending billions of dollars to help people all over the world. Let's spend a little to help a boy right here at home take care of his dog." He dropped a dollar bill into his hat and handed it to the man next to him, who also dropped a dollar into the hat and passed it on.

A few minutes later the hat returned to the truck driver, who emptied all the bills and coins from it. He squeezed the fistful of money tightly and then put it into the boy's hand. The boy looked at the people in amazement. He could hardly believe the money was for him. Then he breathed a fervent, "Thank you, mister, and thanks to everybody too. Now maybe my dog has a chance to live."

JANALEE'S BEST PRESENT

Janalee and her family lived in Oregon. One day when Janalee was only seven she went to Primary. The lesson in her class was on baptism.

That night Janalee told her family that when she became eight years of age, all she wanted for a birthday present was to be baptized. Her father said he would not let her join any church until she was much older than eight and really understood what she was doing.

Her mother knew how disappointed Janalee was. She tried to comfort her and encouraged her to be patient. She suggested they pray together often and ask that her father might come to know how much this meant to his little girl.

Janalee's eighth birthday came, but she did not receive the present for which she had asked.

Soon afterward her family moved into a lonely valley sixty-five miles from town. One day her mother found Janalee playing Primary with her little sisters, Jeredee and Jones, and her brother, Eddy. The next Sunday she suggested to their father that the family hold their own worship meeting. He agreed and joined in the songs and prayers.

A few days later he went back to the town where the family had previously lived. He called on the Primary president. He talked with the missionaries. Then he began to study.

Janalee's best present didn't come to her on her eighth birthday. She received it one Saturday night several nights later when she and her family drove sixty-five miles from their home back to the place where she had first attended Primary. It came to her in the never-to-be-forgotten moment when the elder called her name just after she had watched her daddy be baptized.

ONE BOY KNEW

The class was restless. It seemed as if the day had been unusually long, and the boys were eager to be out of school and free to finish the game they had started during the noon recess. The cool Scottish afternoon had almost ended, and there would be little time to play before the daily fog rolled in over the schoolyard, hiding the sun.

The teacher had promised that they would be excused early if they could quickly copy a prayer that she was writing on the blackboard for them to take home and memorize. She explained that she thought it was a beautiful one, and she urged the students to think about every word as they copied so the prayer would have a special meaning for each one.

It was quiet in the rooom except for the squeak of the teacher's chalk and the boys' pencils as she wrote and they copied: "Teach us, good Lord, to serve thee as thou deservest; to give and not to count the cost; to fight and not to seed the wounds; to toil and not to seek for rest; to labor and not to ask for any reward except that of knowing that we do thy will. Amen."

As she finished writing and chalked in the last period, the teacher turned to the class and asked,

"Isn't this a good prayer, boys?" Then without waiting for an answer, she added, "It must have been written by someone who was willing to keep on working for others without ever being tired and without thinking of getting any pay for doing so. As you memorize it, try to think about who this could be."

The boys hurriedly put away their pencils and notebooks, most of them thinking only of getting out-of-doors and starting with the game. But each one paused thoughtfully for a moment when one boy raised his hand and commented quietly, "I already know. It could have been written by my mother."

RUTH'S HIKE

The wagon party turned away from the trail it had followed along the Platte River. The ground was rougher than it had looked from a distance, but the travelers had no choice but to cross the smelly alkali sinks with their poison waters. Skeletons of the cattle that had died from the water were strewn along the way.

When the group neared the Sweetwater River, willow and cherry trees lined the banks of the stream, and a valley opened out. Thirteen-year-old Ruth, walking beside her father's ox team, thought it was the prettiest sight she had ever seen.

Ahead a huge granite mass loomed high in the air. How glad everyone was to see this famous landmark, Independence Rock, where most of the pioneers and trappers of the West stopped to write their names in red, yellow, or black paint or to leave messages for those they knew would soon pass that way. A few shrubs and one small lonely pine marked an opening partway up where thirty or forty people could stand and look out on every side over the prairie.

Although all in the wagon party were tired and

needed rest, many of the men and children and some of the women too were soon scaling the huge rock to read the names written there or to add their own names. Some went just to look out over the land to the east from where they had come and to the west where they were going. Ruth eagerly hiked to the very top of Independence Rock where she carefully chiseled her name in large letters: RUTH MAY, 1867.

It was an exciting moment for the young girl, who with her father had journeyed from England and who had walked all the way across the plains. But she could never have dreamed of a moment sixty-four years later when, as the third president of the Young Women's Mutual Improvement Association, seventy-seven-year-old Ruth May Fox would again climb the huge granite mass after taking part in the unveiling of a pioneer marker on Independence Rock, Wyoming.

In fact, she could not have foreseen that the YWMIA would be organized by Brigham Young in November 1869 and that in the following years girls throughout the world would find growth and joy in its many programs and activities.

TWO CLOCKS

It was the first warm night of early summer. Dawn would soon light the sky above the eastern mountains, bringing a fresh breeze from the canyon. But at the moment the house was stifling, and Lawrence, Sandra, Raymond, and Ruann stirred restlessly in their beds.

The night before they had offered a special prayer for Dad, who had been taken back to the hospital, and for Mom, who could always smile even though Dad had had one bad sick spell after another the past several years. She had assured the children that everything would be all right, but Lawrence, who was twelve, caught a worried look on her face when she didn't know anyone was looking at her. The boy had slept and awakened and dozed and then awakened all through the night.

Lawrence knew it would take Mom some time to get dressed and drive nearly fifteen miles to the Salt Lake hospital from their home. "What's the matter, Mom?" he asked. Then almost before she could answer, he went on, "What can I do to help?"

Mom explained that Dad was desperately ill and needed her. She sent Lawrence for Grandma, who

31

lived nearby and then hurriedly kissed him good-bye as she fairly flew out the door and into the car.

When Grandma arrived, Lawrence and the other children were all sitting in the front room wide-eyed and worried. Quickly they knelt down, and fervent prayers were given by each one in turn, even by three-year-old Ruann. As they arose, the clock on the mantle chimed five o'clock.

Meanwhile at the hospital the nurses had hurried Dad into surgery. They explained to Mom when she got there that he had started hemorrhaging, that nothing they had done had helped, and that the doctor said only an operation might save his life.

Mom expected a long wait, but in a few minutes the doctor came out of surgery looking puzzled. He walked up to her, shook his head in disbelief, and said, "I don't understand, but all at once the bleeding stopped. We won't need to operate. It seems almost like a miracle."

Mom breathed a silent prayer of gratitude as she looked up at the hospital clock. It was exactly 5 a.m.

A BABY'S BLESSING

Six-month-old Carol lay on the bed kicking and stretching. Her sister, Marilyn, who was five years old, had promised Mother she would watch her carefully and was proud she was old enough to help.

Right in the middle of a happy squeal, baby Carol gave a hard kick and rolled off the bed. Mother came running when she heard a loud thud followed by cries of the children. She picked both children up at once and tried to quiet them.

But baby Carol did not stop crying. Her little hands kept tugging at her hair. She would not take her bottle nor eat her food.

When Marilyn, who hovered close all day, touched her, the baby's head felt hot, and her eyes seemed to roll back in her head.

Marilyn's mother called a doctor. After examining the baby, he said that when Carol fell off the bed, she had hit her head so hard she had suffered a brain concussion. He told the worried family what to do and promised to call again in a few days.

Marilyn's heart was heavy. She felt the accident had somehow been her fault even though her mother and father both told her over and over again that they did not blame her.

Marilyn, however, could not be comforted at all. Whenever she heard her beloved little sister whimper as if she were in pain, she felt like crying too.

Several days went by. The baby did not eat and hardly slept at all. The family decided to ask the bishopric to come and bless little Carol. Mother and Marilyn silently joined in the prayer that was given.

Almost at the very moment the men finished praying, the baby stopped crying. She looked around, smiled at Marilyn, and then for the first time in days went quietly to sleep.

An hour later the doctor came to Marilyn's home. He examined Carol carefully and then said, "This is most surprising. Your baby shows no symptoms of brain concussion at all. She seems normal in every way."

THE BEST SPORT

Even before the coach announced the date of try-outs for the Little League baseball team, Bobby had spent hours practicing. He practiced whenever he could find someone else who wanted to play ball. When there was no one, Bobby exercised to build up his muscles and worked to earn money to buy the Little League shoes the coach had suggested would help a boy play better ball.

In fact, all Bobby was interested in that spring was making the team. He had been on a neighborhood team for two years, and this was his last chance to become a Little Leaguer.

It was exciting for Bobby's family when he and his younger brother, Chris, were chosen in the final group of twenty boys. From them fifteen would be picked to make up the Little League team.

Bobby was sure no other boy had worked harder or was more eager than he to become a member of the team. So it was a shock when the coach called his name as one of the five boys to be dropped.

Chris, who had won a place on the team, loyally told Bobby, "If you can't play, I won't be on the team either."

"Sure, you will," answered Bobby. "It's okay."

Bobby was at every game that summer cheering for Chris and the other boys. He even loaned Chris the baseball shoes he had worked so hard to earn and helped the team members sell candy to earn extra money for their new equipment.

Bobby thought no one knew how disappointed or how lonely and left out he sometimes felt.

Then one day as the boys were riding home with their parents after a game, Father started to recite a part of Kipling's poem "If":

If you can make one heap of all your winnings;
And risk it on one turn of pitch-and-toss;
And lose, and start again at your beginnings
And never breathe a word about your loss . . .

And Mother continued:

Yours is the Earth, and everything that's in it,
And—which is more—you'll be a man, my son.

Bobby looked first at his father and then at his mother. He felt a lump come into his throat, but his eyes were shining as he smiled at his father and then squeezed his mother's hand.

BIRTHDAY BAPTISM

When Alice's mother and sisters decided to become members of The Church of Jesus Christ of Latter-day Saints, Alice was only six and too young to be baptized with the rest of her family. They often talked of the wonderful experience of baptism and their joy at being members of the Church.

For weeks before her birthday all Alice could think about was her dream of being baptized on the day she turned eight. "Not sometime after," she said, "but on the very day."

Then on the morning of the third day before her birthday, Alice awakened with a severe headache. The next day she was too ill to go to school, and the doctor told her mother he was afraid she would be in bed at least a week.

Alice's big eyes filled with tears of disappointment. The day before her birthday she was worse, but most of all she hurt all over with disappointment at not being able to be baptized as she had hoped. Her temperature rose even higher that day despite the medicine that the doctor had prescribed and that her mother gave every few hours.

Alice's Primary teacher told the rest of the story in a letter:

As the mother came into the sickroom on the afternoon of the day before Alice's birthday, she found the girl kneeling on her bed fervently praying. It seems the girl was wrestling for fulfillment of her desire. The mother did not disturb the child and left the room, affected.

On the next morning, her eighth birthday, Alice got up, dressed, and prepared for baptism. She was without a fever now. Some hours later the mother used the thermometer once more, and it showed no alteration. So God had accepted the prayer of this child.

On the afternoon of Alice's eighth birthday she was baptized. She was well, happy—and thankful!

BOBBY'S CHRISTMAS GIFT

It was only two weeks until Christmas, and in most homes there were lights and laughter and joy. But in Bobby's home there was only sadness. His father was dead, and both his grandmother and his mother were too sick to work and too poor to provide for any Christmas.

Bobby decided to send a letter to the newspaper about the matter. Among other things he wrote: "I'm a little boy six years old. I live with my mother and grandmother. They are sick. I'm praying that Santa will bring us something to eat and something to wear."

Although Bobby's letter was printed in the *Lethbridge Herald,* it was copied by many other newspapers. One of them reached a home in Utah where Jack lived with his grandmother, who read the letter to him. Jack's father was far away in the army, and his mother had died a few months before.

Jack often felt lost and lonely, even though he loved Granny and she was good to him. He knew she had tried to think of some way to interest Jack in holiday plans, but how could he care about Christmas without Dad or Mother? Even Granny didn't seem to know how sad he felt inside all of the time.

Jack kept thinking about the letter Bobby had written. He was sure he knew exactly how the other boy felt, and he wanted so much to do something to help. Then he remembered his favorite suit. Mother had bought it for him a few months before she died. It was almost too small now, and Granny had carefully put it away for him to keep.

Jack decided to send it to Bobby. He began to think of other things he could send too, and the more he thought the more excited he became.

At first Granny didn't think that Jack should give away this special suit. But when he explained that he just knew Mother would want him to do so, Granny agreed.

Together they wrapped a box of clothes and toys and mailed it that very day to Canada. Jack enclosed a letter that explained about the suit and ended by saying: "I'm a little American boy. I'm six years old too and live with my grandmother. My daddy is one of Uncle Sam's soldiers. I hope you will have a good Christmas."

Many people who read Bobby's letter sent food and clothes and toys to him that Christmas, but his favorite gifts were those that came from Jack in America. The *Lethbridge Herald* reported in an article December 25th that "little Bobby's prayer has been answered."

Almost a thousand miles away Christmas morning dawned clear and cold outside the little house where Jack and his grandmother lived. But inside their hearts was a shining warmth as Jack thought about how he had helped to bring Christmas joy to his unknown friend, Bobby, in Canada.

THE BOXER

The very air seemed to tingle with excitement in the gym of the New York Athletic Club. It was time for the big event of the evening. Both fighters were tough, well-trained, and eager to win, and almost all the boys who filled the benches were cheering for their favorite boxer.

The referee gave his instructions and warnings. As the timer's bell sounded, the favorite boxer of nearly all the boys paused for just a moment with his head bowed before dancing into the ring. It was apparent to everyone that he was praying, and a momentary hush came over the crowded gymnasium.

It was an exciting bout, and after it was over one of the fight officials asked the boxer why he had stopped to pray at a time like that. "Did you think it would help you win?" he asked.

"Of course not," answered the young winner. "I was praying for three things. First, I prayed that I wouldn't get hurt bad. Then I prayed that I wouldn't kill or cripple the other guy. But I prayed most of all because my mom has told me I could help kids see that everyone needs to pray, even a tough boxer."

SHINING MOMENTS
IN THE LIVES
OF CHURCH PRESIDENTS

A PROMISE

It was on a frosty morning in the winter of 1831 that a sleigh stopped in front of a store in Kirtland, Ohio. A handsome young man threw back the buffalo robe that covered his knees and those of the other men and a woman who were with him. He sprang down from the sleigh and walked quickly into the store.

The man behind the counter was surprised when the young stranger stretched out his hand and said, "Newel K. Whitney, thou art the man!"

The storekeeper had never seen the young man before and stammered, "I'm sorry, sir, but I don't seem to be able to place you."

"I'm Joseph the Prophet," was the unexpected reply. "You've prayed me here. Now what do you want of me?"

Newel K. Whitney and his wife had been praying to know which church to join. They knew the arrival of Joseph Smith was an answer to that prayer and soon became members of The Church of Jesus Christ of Latter-day Saints.

A short time later, Newel left his store to go with the Prophet to visit other Church members. As they were returning to Kirtland by stagecoach, the horses became frightened, and Newel was caught in a wheel and received a badly broken leg and foot. They were some distance from home, and Joseph stayed nearly a month with his friend to nurse him back to health.

In the area were many who were bitter enemies of the Mormons and especially of the Prophet, and they tried to kill him by putting poison in the food. In telling of this later Joseph said:

> One day when I rose from the dinner table, I walked directly to the door and commenced vomiting most profusely. I raised large quantities of blood and poisonous matter, and so great were the muscular contortions of my system, that my jaw in a few moments was dislocated. This I succeeded in replacing with my own hands and made my way to Bro. Whitney (who was on the bed), as speedily as possible; he laid his hands on me and administered to me in the name of the Lord, and I was healed, in an instant.

The friends decided to leave, but Newel hesitated because he had not used his broken foot for nearly four weeks. Joseph promised him that they would be blessed: a wagon would be waiting to take them to a small river where a ferryboat would be ready to take them across, then a carriage would be waiting to take them to the boat landing where a steamer would be ready to take them up the river.

Early the next morning they left their room. Joseph had had no opportunity to make arrangements for their travel, but a wagon waited outside their door. Just as the Prophet had been led to promise his friend, a ferryboat waited at the river bank, then a carriage was on the other side, and finally a steamer was at the boat landing.

CHIEF KANOSH ENTERTAINS

It was an unusually warm day in early summer when Brigham Young traveled to southern Utah for a visit with Sally and her husband, Chief Kanosh.

Sally, when a small Indian baby, had been captured from her tribe by another tribe and severely mistreated. While still a little girl, she was given to Brigham Young and became a part of his household. When Sally grew older, she married Chief Kanosh, who took her to his tribe in southern Utah.

Sally had liked living in Brigham Young's home. After her marriage she could not get used to keeping house in a tent, so some white friends built her a little cottage. It had windows and a door, and inside were six chairs and a high bed. Chief Kanosh preferred his old wigwam, but on special occasions he would stay temporarily in the house to please Sally.

Brigham Young had befriended many Indians, often sharing food and clothing when they called at his home in Salt Lake City or whenever he met them on his journeys. He had been invited to visit Sally and Chief Kanosh. He thought they would eagerly welcome him as soon as his carriage stopped at their door, but no one came out to greet him.

He waited a few minutes and then sent a messenger to announce his arrival. The chief sent back this word, "Bigham, Bigham sat still in his house, and what is manners for Bigham is manners for Kanosh."

"He's right" was Brigham Young's reply, and he climbed out of his carriage and went into the house.

Some years later one of Brigham Young's daughters recalled this incident in these words: "Father found Kanosh seated like Solomon in all his glory—cross-legged in the middle of the four-poster bed. He wore a heavy overcoat buttoned to the chin, a pair of new boots, and a gorgeous red blanket over all. And this in spite of the fact that it was a very warm day in May. Chief Kanosh sat erect and motionless in all his dignity, and Father attempted to maintain at least a comparative dignity."

President Young enjoyed telling his family of this pleasant visit to his Indian friends.

His never-failing kind treatment of the Indians prompted one chief to say, "What the other white men say goes in one ear and out the other, but what Brigham Young says goes to the heart and stays there."

A MOUNTAIN CELEBRATION

The 24th of July dawned hot and clear. There was not a single cloud in the blue sky overhead nor in the minds of the 2,687 men, women, and children who were guests of Brigham Young at Silver Lake in Big Cottonwood Canyon. They were there to celebrate the tenth anniversary of their safe arrival in the Salt Lake Valley. The year was 1857. For ten years these pioneers had enjoyed peace and prosperity in the beautiful valley of the mountains.

A campground had been prepared on the shores of a small lake, and three boweries had been built so that programs and dancing could be enjoyed. Five bands and numerous choirs had been invited to participate in the "Pioneer Jubilee."

The people had morning prayers in their individual tents and then gathered at sunrise for the raising of a large United States flag in the middle of the campground. Later that morning a special tribute was given to fifty boys between ten and twelve years of age who paraded in brightly colored uniforms. They were called "The Hope of Israel." During the happy hours of the day, laughter and the sounds of merry-making rang throughout the camp.

Then suddenly four hot, dusty horsemen rode up the mountain trail, dismounted quickly, and hurried into Brigham Young's tent. A quietness replaced the noise. Even the smaller children stopped their play and crept close to their fathers and mothers.

In the tent President Young learned that a U.S. army of 2,500 men was marching toward Salt Lake City at that very moment to take over the government of the people, who might be driven from their homes. The army was the result of wicked lies about a Utah rebellion that enemies of the Mormons had persuaded the president of the United States were true. President Young decided to wait until the festivities were over before making an announcement.

Many hours later, when the celebration was winding down, Brigham Young called the people together and told them about the army. The day, which had been one of happiness, suddenly turned into one of fear. Brigham Young reminded the gathering that in 1847 he had promised that "if our enemies will let us alone for ten years, we will ask no odds of them"— and that the ten years had passed. "All will be well," he assured them.

Even the children knew that they might be faced with many problems in the future, but in a shining moment in the beautiful mountains surrounding Salt Lake City everyone knew too that the promise Brigham Young had made as a prophet of God would be fulfilled.

BROWN VELVET

Clarissa Smith was a girl who lived in Salt Lake City not long after the Mormon pioneers settled it in 1847. Her two best friends were Maimie and Josephine Young.

One day when the girls were together, Josephine and Maimie were called from their play and told they were to meet their father. Clarissa was given permission to go with them. This was an exciting occasion because the meeting place was ZCMI, the biggest store in the new pioneer city. Clarissa could hardly wait for them to get there so she could look at the beautiful piece goods on the shelves and dream about a new dress or coat she might have some day.

Brigham Young greeted his two daughters and their friend when they arrived. He took them into the store.

"Let me see that brown velvet, please," he said to the storekeeper. The bolt was lifted down from the shelf, and the material was spread out on the counter. Clarissa thought it was the most beautiful cloth she had ever seen.

"Measure off a piece long enough to make cloaks

for Maimie and Josephine," their father directed the storekeeper.

Then he looked at the other little girl.

"Cut off another length for Clarissa." Brigham Young smiled down at her. "And please make it a very generous one," he said.

THE GOLD WATCH

"Hurry," called Ruth's older brother as he sat in the big white-top wagon waiting for her and their parents to drive from their farm in Idaho to the tabernacle in Logan thirty miles away to hear John Taylor, third president of The Church of Jesus Christ of Latter-day Saints. No one in the family had ever seen or heard President Taylor, but many times Ruth had heard the story of his gold watch.

Five hours later as she sat with her family in the Logan tabernacle, she thought again about the watch and remembered that one of her cousins who lived in Salt Lake had actually seen it.

A special invitation had been given for children in the area to attend this meeting with their parents. Every bench was filled, and many boys and men gladly stood to see and hear this tall bearded man with the melodious voice.

He told how on that fateful afternoon of June 27, 1844, he and Willard Richards were with the Prophet Joseph Smith and his brother Hyrum on the second floor room of Carthage Jail. They had been taken there after being falsely accused of treason and inciting a riot.

The day was warm, and the men were restless. One of them suggested that John sing the hymn "A Poor Wayfaring Man of Grief." As he finished singing, he saw a number of armed men with painted faces rush around the jail. They were followed by a mob of men who raced up the stairs, fired a shot to break the lock on the door, pushed the door open, and then fired another shot that struck Hyrum in the face. As Hyrum fell, the Prophet Joseph bent over him and cried, "Oh, my poor dear brother Hyrum."

John Taylor tried to ward off the attackers with a heavy walking stick that had been left in the room, and then he turned and ran to the window. Before he could leap, however, a shot struck him in the thigh, and another came through the window and would have entered his chest but instead hit a gold watch in his vest pocket. That saved his life. Three more bullets struck him, spattering his blood upon the walls and floor.

When the Prophet Joseph, first president of the Church, was struck dead by bullets and fell out the window, the mob scattered. Later, Dr. Richards, who had not been hit by bullets, dragged John into an inner cell and covered him with an old mattress for protection.

As President Taylor told the tragic story and held up his gold watch for all to see, the huge audience in the tabernacle seemed hardly to breathe.

Ruth often told of the day she saw John Taylor's gold watch and how he stood for hours after the meeting to shake hands with every child who crowded around him.

WILFORD THE FAITHFUL

Two large trees were sprawled on the ground, and Wilford swung his ax again and again as he cut down the third one needed to finish the little cabin at Winter Quarters.

As the tree began to sway, Wilford stepped back away from its fall. However, a crook in the tree twisted it unexpectedly to one side. As it fell, it caught Wilford, knocked him back, and pinned him tightly against a large oak tree, injuring him severely.

Though his breastbone and three ribs were broken and his left thigh, hip, and arm were crushed, he finally managed to get free. The pain was intense, but the only way he could get help was to mount his horse and ride two-and-a-half miles over a narrow rough road back to the settlement at Winter Quarters. Pain shot through his body like an arrow with each step of the horse.

Just outside the little community, Wilford was met by Brigham Young, who helped the injured man off his horse and carefully carried him to his wagon. Before placing him on the wagon bed, several of the men who had gathered around laid their hands upon him and in the name of the Lord rebuked the pain. They promised Wilford that he would live and would help the Saints travel west to find a place where they could worship God according to the dictates of their own conscience.

The year was 1846. Nine months later it was Wilford Woodruff's wagon that carried President Brigham Young when he first looked over the Salt Lake Valley and declared, "This is the place."

Wilford Woodruff was one of the first and greatest missionaries of the Church and was known as "Wilford the Faithful." He became the fourth president of The Church of Jesus Christ of Latter-day Saints, where he served until his death nine years later in 1898.

THE TRAIN RIDE

It was almost time for the train to leave Salt Lake City, and how Rebecca dreaded climbing aboard it to return to her home in Logan—almost a day's journey away. She had not felt this way while waiting to get on the train at Logan the week before. Then there had been nothing but excitement and joy because she had been invited to go with her father and mother to Salt Lake to see the capstone of the Salt Lake Temple put in place.

But the train she took the morning she left Logan had seemed to stagger down the track as it swayed from side to side. It hadn't gone many miles before excitement changed to dizziness and Rebecca's head started to ache. Mother noticed how pale Rebecca had become and suggested that she lie down on the seat, but Rebecca grew worse. The ride to Salt Lake had turned into a sick nightmare she never wanted to repeat.

A big crowd was waiting at the station to board the train. Everyone was talking about the thrilling meeting that had been held the day before at the temple. Rebecca had been proud to be there and remembered still the warm excitement of the day, but mostly all she could think about was her fear of being sick again on the train. She gulped all the fresh cool air she could and decided she'd rather walk to Logan than ever get on a train again, but of course she knew she couldn't do that.

Just as the train was ready to pull out of the station, Lorenzo Snow came hurrying into the car. Rebecca had heard her father say he would probably be the next president of the Church and that he surely would become the first president of the Salt Lake Temple. He was a kindly looking man with his long white beard and pleasant expression.

Every seat in the car was taken, and Brother Snow stood looking up and down. Rebecca's father motioned to him and urged Mother to squeeze closer so that Brother Snow could sit with them.

"Oh, dear," thought Rebecca. "How awful it will be if I'm sick with Brother Snow sitting near." She murmured a quiet but desperate prayer that she might not disgrace herself and her family and that her stomach would behave at least until the train arrived at Brigham City, where Brother Snow lived.

Brother Snow greeted others in the car as he made his way to the seat next to Rebecca. As he smiled gratefully, there washed over Rebecca the sweet assurance that if she could sit close to Brother Snow, she would be blessed all the way to Logan.

"I'll sit close to your little girl," Brother Snow told Rebecca's father. "I'm sure we'll have a pleasant ride."

He sat down, patted Rebecca's shoulder, and then smiled at her as if he understood exactly what her problem was. "It will be a good ride, my dear," he promised.

And it was!

THE SURVIVOR

The sea was very rough in the mouth of the little harbor of Lahaina, Hawaii, but the men in the ship anchored in the channel had great need of going ashore. It was finally decided that Elder Joseph F. Smith, a young Mormon elder, should stay on board with all the suitcases and books while the other four elders climbed into a small boat with the ship's captain and started for shore.

Joseph, watching from the ship's deck, was filled with horror when he saw a giant wave hit the boat and capsize it in the foaming surf.

Some natives rowed out from shore, pulled four of the men from the water, and started for land. Elder W. W. Cluff, one of the survivors, demanded that they return and find Elder Lorenzo Snow, whom they could not see. A frantic search was made, and it was nearly twenty minutes later that the body was brought to the surface by a native.

Elder Lorenzo Snow, stiff and apparently lifeless, was laid across the laps of Elder Alma Smith and Elder Cluff, who administered to him and prayed with all their hearts that he might live.

On the sandy beach were several large empty barrels. The body of Elder Snow was placed face downward on one of the barrels, and his companions rolled him back and forth until all the water he had swallowed was squeezed out of him.

This all happened in March 1864—many years before the development of mouth-to-mouth resuscitation—but that night Elder Cluff wrote in his diary: "Finally we were impressed to place our mouth over his and make an effort to inflate his lungs. After a little, we received very faint indications of returning life. These grew more and more distinct until consciousness was fully restored."

On September 13, 1893, Lorenzo Snow became the fifth president of The Church of Jesus Christ of Latter-day Saints. The young man, Elder Joseph F. Smith, who watched the accident from the ship's deck, succeeded President Snow and became sixth president of the Church.

A SLEIGH RIDE SURPRISE

Snow lay deep over Salt Lake Valley. When the children became tired of playing in it, they would dare each other to wait for a sleigh to come by and to catch a ride on its runners.

The most beautiful sleigh in all the valley was one owned by Brigham Young. Nearly every afternoon he would go for a ride in it while his coachman guided a fine team of horses over the frozen ground.

Six-year-old Heber often watched this sleigh and dreamed of someday riding on its runners. They stuck out so far behind the rest of the carriage that he thought they would make a perfect place on which to stand and ride.

One day as he watched the sleigh, it slowed down to go around a corner. Heber was so close to it, he was able to jump on the runners before it began to speed up again.

At first it was exciting to ride through the crisp air as the horses tossed their heads and the sleigh bells tinkled merrily. Heber thought he would go only a few blocks and then, when the horses slowed down, he would hop off and hurry home.

But the animals did not slacken their speed. They

ran swiftly through the town and into the country. Heber was nearly breathless as the bitter wind and snow whirled around him. His teeth chattered with cold and fear as he prayed that he might get back home safely. He shivered at the thought of what Brigham Young might say and do if he found a boy riding on the runners of his sleigh.

When the horses had gone more than five miles, they came to a frozen stream and at last slowed down to make their way across it. Heber jumped off and started racing back toward town. He had gone only a short way when he heard a voice boom out, "Stop! Stop, little boy! You are about frozen. Come get warm under my buffalo robe, and then we'll take you home."

This moment was one Heber J. Grant never forgot. It was his first meeting with Brigham Young, the second president of The Church of Jesus Christ of Latter-day Saints.

MY LITTLE MEN

Thomas E. was only five and David O. was just past seven. Their father, David McKay, had been called to go on a mission to Scotland. Their little sister, Jeanette, was barely three, and Mother was soon to have another baby.

It was hard for Father to make plans to leave his family, for he knew how much they needed him. Yet the call had come to go, and he felt he could not refuse.

The boys sensed how difficult it was for their father to know what he should do. They often talked together and wished they were men and could do all his work so he would feel happy about leaving them. They knew there was much to be done around the farm if Father went away. The animals would have to be fed and tended, the cows milked, wood chopped and carried, and dozens of other chores completed.

One evening as they all knelt around the supper table for family prayer, Father suggested that he ask the Church authorities to postpone his mission until spring crops could be planted and the new baby born.

The boys looked up, feeling young and helpless.

"No," said Mother firmly, "your call is for April

and you must go!" Then she looked gravely at Thomas E. and David O. and said, "My little men will see that we get along all right."

Neither boy ever forgot the thrill of that moment or the solemn promise they made then, "We'll help you, Mother."

Father left for his mission in April.

A PERFECT VISIT

It had been an exciting visit, the first one ever made to Samoa by an apostle. Long rowboats decorated with colorful garlands of vines and flowers had met the boat when David O. McKay and Hugh J. Cannon arrived.

A Mormon band greeted the rowboats at the wharf and proudly escorted the visitors to a circle where all the chiefs of the islands waited to welcome them with speeches and the kava drink ceremony. Then a great feast was enjoyed under a coconut leaf canopy, and many people brought their children and their sick ones to be blessed.

During the following week meetings had been held on the various islands, and now the last morning was to be spent with the children in the school at Sauniatu.

This was May 31, 1921—thirty years before David O. McKay became president of the Church—but he often referred to the day as one of the most memorable of his life. That night he wrote about it in his diary:

As we came out of the school, we found the people standing in double column from our door out across the lawn to the street.

Finally, the last little boy crowding around had pressed our hands, so with tear-bedimmed eyes, we walked slowly toward the stream beyond which our horses were waiting. The band on the porch played "Tofa, My Feleni" and the people stood waving their farewell. Before we were ready to start, they gathered around us again eager to have one more handshake.

As we rode slowly away, the band leading, the people followed as if they just would not yield to parting. We had gone perhaps a quarter of a mile ahead of them when I felt impressed to say, "I think we should return and leave our blessing with them here in this beautiful grove."

As we approached the sobbing crowd, I could not help thrilling with the scene.

Hanging my folded umbrella on an overhanging limb of a kopoc tree, I dismounted. The sobs of the people were louder than my voice when I began to pray, but they became more subdued as I continued, and their *Amene* was distinct and impressive at the close.

Oh, I never will forget you, *Samoa e galo atu.*

I DID IT!

A little breeze stirred the warm noon air. The choir had sung the closing hymn, and a crowd had gathered behind the Salt Lake Tabernacle to see the man they acknowledged as their prophet leave the building after that morning session of general conference.

Men, women, and children pressed against the ropes that marked the way he would come. A few jockeyed for a better place to see him, for a closer spot where they might even reach out a hand to touch his clothing as he went by.

A three-year-old girl with long black curls clung close to her Mexican mother, her big eyes alive with love as her sweet voice was heard above the murmur of the crowd, "I'd like to kiss President McKay."

An elderly woman turned to her husband and questioned, "Who wouldn't?"

A few minutes later on the arms of two friends, President McKay walked slowly out of the dome-shaped building and made his way through the roped corridor, smiling and nodding to those who had gathered in his honor.

The eager child, in a colorful Mexican dress,

squirmed loose from her mother, stooped under the ropes, and threw her arms tightly around the legs of the white-haired prophet.

President McKay stopped, looked down at the face turned so eagerly up toward his, and pulled his arms free from those who were walking with him. He leaned over, lifted the little girl, and held her close to his heart. The breeze picked up one of her black curls and blew it against his white hair as he stood straight and tall with her in his arms. She looked lovingly into the eyes that smiled back at her.

Quickly her little hands cupped his face as her lips brushed his cheek. He held her a moment longer, then gently lowered her to her feet. Through misty eyes, those close by saw an especially radiant smile light his face as he was helped into his car.

There was a momentary hush as the little girl ran back under the ropes to her mother. No one stirred. No one spoke. The stillness was broken by a small voice that almost reverently and with awed wonderment exclaimed, "Mommy, I did it!"

A SPECIAL BIRTHDAY PRESENT

It was a warm autumn day in Salt Lake City, and the neighborhood children were all enjoying the last few days before the beginning of school. Ruth Ann and her friend had spent the morning under a big shade tree playing with their dolls and talking.

At lunch that noon, Ruth Ann asked her mother, "Why didn't you tell me that today is President McKay's birthday? He is our very own neighbor, and I'd have given him a present."

"I'm sorry, Ruth Ann," her mother answered. "I thought you had heard us talking about him being seventy-nine years old today." Then she smiled as she added, "But I wouldn't worry about a present for him. He'll receive so many that he probably wouldn't even know it if you did give him one."

Ruth Ann ate her lunch in thoughtful silence. A few minutes later Mother looked out the window in time to see Ruth Ann and Sandy talking earnestly about something. They stopped by a bed of fall flowers in brilliant bloom. But it was nearly two weeks later before she thought again of the incident. That was the evening the telephone rang and a woman's voice asked, "Do you have a daughter named Ruth

Ann? I have a letter for her and want to be sure it reaches the right little girl."

The very next day the mailman brought an envelope with two letters inside it. One letter was for Sandy and the other was for Ruth Ann. Ruth Ann, who was only eight and couldn't read it all by herself, listened with growing excitement as her mother began:

> Dear Miss Barker and Miss Davis:
> When Sister McKay and I returned from Los Angeles last evening, we found awaiting us some flowers and a box of peaches with a note "from Ruth Ann Barker and Sandra Davis—Happy Birthday." Whether you sent the flowers or the peaches, we do not know, so we are thanking you for both. . . .

As mother continued to read the letter to Ruth Ann, the girl's eyes grew big and bright in delighted wonderment that a great and busy man would take the time to write to two girls who had remembered his birthday.

The letter was signed, "David O. McKay, president of The Church of Jesus Christ of Latter-day Saints."

THE BIRTHDAY PICNIC

The picnic had not been planned because of the birthday. In fact, the children did not even know it was his birthday, nor did the teacher think of it when her Sunday School class decided they would have a picnic near the birthplace of the prophet.

The picnic was to be held on Saturday, and Friday the mother of one of the children called the teacher to remind her of the prophet's birthday the next day.

"Do you suppose he'll be visiting there?" the mother asked. "Sometimes he goes back home for his birthday, you know."

The teacher called his office and was told that he was indeed going there the next day, that many members of the family might be traveling with him, and that the children could not hope to see him. "In fact," said the secretary, "tomorrow wouldn't be a good day for you to take that many boys and girls anywhere near his home."

It was too late to cancel the picnic, so the teacher bought a dozen roses just to leave on the porch of the prophet's house, and Saturday morning the eager children loaded into cars for the forty-mile drive.

The early autumn sun was warm, but a cool

canyon breeze reminded the happy group that summer was over. Red and gold leaves topped some of the sheer rock walls of Ogden Canyon. As the cars drove around Pine View Dam and then into the green Huntsville valley, the children seemed to have forgotten that they would not see the prophet.

"Maybe he'll go by in his car," said one.

"He might see us and wave," suggested another.

The picnic lunch was eaten in a little park, and then the cars drove to a white two-story home surrounded by a white fence and shaded by tall poplar trees. Just as they arrived, a big black limousine came up the street and stopped. In wide-eyed wonder the children watched as President McKay carefully helped his frail wife out of the car and walked hand in hand with her through the gate and into the house.

A short time later their teacher carried the roses up the path and gave them to a man on the porch, explaining they were a birthday gift from twenty-four eight- and nine-year-olds.

As she turned away, the figure of a man filled the doorway, and the boys and girls heard him call out, "Where are those children? I'd like to see them."

The teacher pointed to the cars, and President McKay motioned for those inside the cars to come onto the lawn. He greeted each one, shook hands with every boy and girl, and expressed his love and appreciation for them. In the eyes of the adoring children, their prophet stood as tall as the snow-covered mountains.

As they rode home, one of the boys who was usually full of mischief and noise expressed the feelings of all when he looked at his grimy, popsicle-streaked hand and said with quiet reverence, "I just wish I'd never have to wash this hand again so I could keep the feel of President McKay's hand on it forever!"

A PROPHET IN ISRAEL

In September 1972 President Harold B. Lee visited Israel. President Lee was accompanied by Sister Lee, Elder Gordon B. Hinckley of the Quorum of the Twelve Apostles, and Sister Hinckley.

While in the Holy Land, President Lee met with the mayor of Jerusalem and other officials of the Israeli government. He also visited Bethlehem, where Jesus was born, and Nazareth, where the Savior spent his childhood.

One of his special visits was to the Garden Tomb, a beautiful area where it is believed Jesus was buried and rose from the dead. There President Lee met with the Saints in Israel and organized the Jerusalem Branch of the Church. The Primary children of the new branch sang one of President Lee's favorite songs—"I Am a Child of God."

Later when President Lee spoke to members of the Church in Rome, he told them that his choicest experience in the Holy Land was hearing the children sing that lovely song. He explained that we all are truly God's children and that our Heavenly Father wants us to do what's right so that we can return to live with him.

The children of the Jerusalem Branch will always remember President Lee and his visit with them. They felt blessed that a modern-day prophet visited their land, where Jesus lived and taught.

SHINING MOMENTS
IN THE LIVES
OF GREAT MEN
AND WOMEN

THE STRANGER

The boy straightened up, twisting and turning as he did so, and rubbed his aching back. All day he had been working with several men to clear the land. He was younger than they and stronger. He looked at them and knew they must be even more tired than he, but there was still work to be done.

"Keep going, you lazy loafer," shouted the corporal in charge. "Nobody's going to stop for anything around here. This timber's got to be cleared for General Washington, and I aim to see that you do it—no matter how long it takes or how you feel." His voice was loud and domineering. All day long he had been giving orders to work harder and faster although each one worked steadily and without complaint.

The boy again bent his back. The man next to him was breathing hard as he tried to lift a heavy piece of timber.

"Come on, you boys, get moving," shouted the corporal. The men and the boy leaned over and tried to lift the heavy log but staggered back under its weight.

The corporal watched them without making a move to help. Just as he started to shout an ugly command to hurry with their work, a man came riding by on horseback.

He stopped and watched only an instant before he turned to the corporal and said, "Why don't you help? Can't you see that the log is too heavy for your men?"

"I'm a corporal—that's not my work," said the officer as he glared at the stranger.

The man on horseback made no reply. Instead he quickly climbed down and quietly assisted the workers. With the extra help, the heavy timber was moved and the other work was soon completed.

The men and the boy started to thank the stranger, but the corporal silenced them. He turned to the man, who had swung easily up into his saddle, but before he could say anything the stranger leaned down, looked straight at the corporal, and said, "Next time you want anything like that done that you feel is beneath you, just call on your commander-in-chief."

With a friendly wave of his hand to the boy and his fellow-workers, the stranger was gone. The men and boy watched in awed silence as General George Washington rode away.

A LETTER TO A HEROINE

Father read the letter while the family crowded around his bed and listened in breathless silence.

Prudence's thoughts went back to the cold day a few months before when her brother, Bob, had come from Valley Forge to spend a day at home. He had told them about the suffering of the soldiers and how they wrapped their feet in rags to keep them warm and protect them from the snow.

Prudence longed to do something to help. The family owned but one thing of value—a diamond brooch that her grandmother had worn when she was presented to the queen of England. The brooch had been given to Prudence a few months before on her ninth birthday.

"You can look at it now and know it is yours," her mother said on that special day, "but Father will keep it locked in his safe until you are eighteen. Then you may wear it."

That had been a happy moment, but nothing like the one that flooded over her when she decided to send the brooch back with Bob so it might be traded for food and shoes for at least a few of the soldiers who were fighting for American independence at Valley Forge.

At first Mother had protested, but Father, who had been ill for many months, called her to his bedside. "I thank God for the loyalty of our little girl," he said. "And it is much more important that men have shoes and food than that a young girl wear a diamond brooch."

Now months later Prudence's eyes glowed as Father again read the letter. His eyes were misty but full of pride as he began, "My brave little heroine." She listened quietly as the letter thanked her for her loyal and generous heart and told of the soldiers she had helped.

Mother held her close as they both looked again at the letter, which closed with the words, "God bless you, my child."

It was signed, "General George Washington."

DR. SPELVIN'S TREASURE

The boy splashed through the rain and mud. He had walked miles from his small cabin home, but he had been so eager to see the treasure Dr. Spelvin owned that his long legs had covered the ground quickly.

He hesitated only a moment before knocking at the door. It was opened almost at once, and the doctor invited the boy to come in out of the cold to warm and dry himself by the open fireplace.

A narrow shelf on the wall across the room held a number of books, and the boy's eyes kept going back and forth across each volume. In all his nine years, he had never seen so many books. He figured there must be more than a dozen!

He thought of the one book there was at home—a well-read Bible—and of how Mr. Criley down at the general store had told him of an exciting one called *Robinson Crusoe*. It was Mr. Criley who had also told the boy that Dr. Spelvin owned this book and others too and that maybe he would loan it for reading. This was why the boy had splashed through mud and rain nearly nine long miles.

Now that he had arrived, he looked at the doctor

and then at the books, not daring to ask if he might borrow one of those precious volumes. Finally the doctor spoke, "Is there someone sick at your place? Is that why you've come so far on this stormy night?"

"Oh, no," the boy answered. "Everybody's all right at home, but . . . " He stopped. He looked again at the books on the narrow shelf. Then the words came tumbling out, asking to borrow a book, promising to take good care of it, and apologizing—all at the same time.

The big doctor looked down at the boy, who thought for a moment that he must surely return home through the rain empty-handed as he had come.

There was a long silence except for the snap of the logs in the fireplace. Then Dr. Spelvin strode across the room, picked up the book *Robinson Crusoe* from the shelf, and handed it to Abraham Lincoln, the boy who had walked eighteen miles all alone on a stormy night to see and borrow Dr. Spelvin's treasure—a book.

THE EXPRESSMAN

Hours before it was time to leave, Dolly had been
ready for her very first all-alone trip on the train. Her
calfskin trunk, studded with brass nails, stood near
the door waiting to be picked up and taken to the railroad station several blocks away. Days ago Mother
had made arrangements for a man to haul it in his
wagon.

Again and again Dolly had run out to the gate to
look up and down the street for him, but for some
reason the expressman had not come. It was almost
train time, and she could not go on the trip without
her trunk.

Mother paced anxiously up and down the parlor,
glancing now and then at the tall grandfather clock
that was ticking away the quickly passing minutes.
There was hardly time left to get to the station before
the train would leave. The trunk was too heavy for
her to carry. What could be done?

Dolly did not want Mother to see her cry, so she
ran out to the gate once more, tears streaking down
her face, just as a tall unusual-looking man walked
by. Seeing her distress, he stopped and asked,
"What's the matter, little girl?"

As Dolly sobbed out her story of disappointment, he gently patted her head. His kind eyes smiled as he leaned over and told her to run into the house to get her mother and tell her he would take care of the trunk. He lifted it up onto his shoulder, urged Dolly to hurry so she wouldn't miss the train, and started up the street.

Mother and Dolly raced to catch the lanky man and then had to almost run the rest of the way to the station to keep up with his long steps. He slipped her small hand into his big one to help her along. There was little time to talk, but a few comments he made as they hurried along made Mother smile and helped Dolly to dry her last tear and to make her forget her last worry.

The trunk was put on the train just as it was ready to pull out of the station. Dolly kissed her mother, climbed on board, and took a seat near the window. The tall man smiled and waved good-bye to her as the train rolled down the tracks.

It was only then that she heard the people around her respectfully call him Mr. Lincoln. A few months later Dolly learned that her "expressman" had been elected president of the United States. She felt a warm thrill as she thought of how this great man had helped her.

GRACE WRITES A LETTER

It was a cold morning, even for February. But despite the chill, a large crowd waited anxiously at the station in Westfield, New York, for the special presidential train to arrive. The air tingled with excitement in anticipation of seeing the man who had been born in a log cabin and who was now on his way to live in the White House.

No one in the crowd was more eager or more excited than eleven-year-old Grace Bedell. Yet she almost dreaded the train's arrival. Although it had seemed just the thing to do at the time, she now wondered how she ever dared write a letter to Abraham Lincoln last fall.

When Mr. Lincoln was first nominated for president, her father said that everyone commented about Mr. Lincoln's looks—his enemies laughed at the idea that such a man could be president, and his friends wished that something could be done to improve his looks. Grace wondered why.

Then one day her father brought home a picture of Mr. Lincoln. Grace had never before seen his photograph, and she was startled at the raw-boned homeliness of the face that seemed to look right at her.

She had turned the picture this way and then that. As she did so, candlelight fell on the photo, making it appear that Mr. Lincoln wore a beard, which seemed to soften his features and make him almost handsome.

The thought came to her that if he knew how much better he looked with a beard, surely he would grow one. Then people would stop talking about his face and would start talking about why they should vote for him.

Finally she wrote a letter to the Springfield lawyer and told him, "You would look a great deal better with a beard because your face is so thin," she had written.

Now four months later Grace stood at the station and wondered how she could ever have been so bold as to write this suggestion to such a man.

The train finally whistled to a stop. More than a thousand people stirred and craned their necks to see the tall gaunt figure who stepped out onto the platform. Grace strained forward on tiptoe, but she could see nothing more than a black hat moving above the crowd. First she was hot, and then she was cold with fear and anticipation.

Then she heard his voice, a thrilling voice that went straight to her heart and made it beat even more wildly.

Mr. Lincoln spoke briefly about loyalty to the nation. Grace's heart almost stopped as she heard him say next, "I have a friend in this place, a little girl who wanted me to be more handsome. If she is present, I would like to speak to Grace Bedell."

The crowd parted as Grace's father led her forward and lifted her onto the platform.

Grace looked up into the kind, sweet face of the president of the United States. Abraham Lincoln reached down and kissed her on both cheeks. Then he stroked his whiskers as he whispered, "Thank you, Grace. You see I let them grow for you!"

A SOLDIER'S DEBT

The young soldier stood at attention before the court.

"William Scott, you have been found guilty," the judge said in a firm voice. "You will be shot by a firing squad within twenty-four hours!"

William's heart was heavy with fear. He was only twenty-two and had joined the Union army a few months earlier to fight for his country.

Two nights before, one of William's comrades had been too sick to do guard duty so William had taken his place. Then the very next night William found himself assigned to guard duty.

The young soldier doubted he could stay awake, and so he went to the captain and told him of his fear. "I'm afraid I can't keep awake on guard duty a second night," William explained. "Could you find a replacement for me?"

The captain was busy, and without really listening, he brushed aside the boy's request.

That night William reported for guard duty, and only a few hours later he was found asleep at his post. Now he was to be shot as a traitor!

As the captain heard the judge pronounce sentence on the young soldier, he stepped forward and pled with the judge. "If anyone ought to be shot," he said, "then I should be the one. Please save William's life."

The sorrow and concern of the captain and the other men of William's regiment for their comrade's life touched the heart of the judge. He thought about the matter for a few minutes, and then he turned to the captain and said softly, "There is only one man who can save your friend. Come, we will go to President Lincoln."

A short time later the judge and captain arrived at the White House. Although the president was very busy, he took time to listen quietly to the story the two men told. When they finished, he said, "It would be a sad thing for a young man like William Scott to die like this."

President Lincoln's voice was full of compassion as he promised, "I will look into the matter myself this very day."

That afternoon the president went to the guard-house of the army camp. He talked with William about his friends back home, his school, and especially about his mother.

"William, you should be thankful that your mother still lives," President Lincoln said gently. "If I were in your place, I would try to make her a proud mother and never cause her any sorrow."

William listened patiently, and then he asked the president a question that had been troubling him. "Would it be possible not to appoint any men from my own regiment to the firing squad?" he asked. "The hardest thing of all would be to die by the hands of my friends."

"My boy," said President Lincoln, "you are not going to be shot tomorrow. I am going to trust you to go back to your regiment. Your country has great need of men like you."

For a moment William could not believe what he had heard, but when he looked into President Lincoln's loving eyes, he knew the words were true. "How can I ever repay you, sir?" he asked in a trembling voice.

President Lincoln put his hands on the young boy's shoulders. "My boy," he said, "my bill is a very large one. No money can pay it, and no friends can help you. There is only one person in all the world who can pay your debt, and his name is William Scott. If you will fight bravely and do your duty as a soldier, then the debt will be paid. Will you make that promise?"

William promised he would do as the president asked. Then with tear-filled eyes, William vowed to himself that with God's help he would keep the solemn promise he made that day to President Abraham Lincoln.

And he did!

TWO BOYS ON A MOUNTAIN

The two boys decided to climb to the top of the rocky mountain. To do so they would have to scale a cliff of lava rock that rose a thousand feet above the basin where they had camped all night.

At first the climb was fairly easy, but then the ledges became narrower. Twice it seemed as if they could not go on. But each time they were almost ready to give up, another thin ledge became apparent, and the boys climbed slowly up the face of the rocky mountain.

When they realized they could not go back the way they had come, there was nothing else to do but go on. Doug, the older of the two, went ahead.

Suddenly the ledge on which Bill was standing began to crumble. He grabbed for a hold above him. Somehow his fingers caught into a narrow slit in the rock, and he found himself hanging by his hands two hundred feet in the air. He yelled for help, but there was no answer. Every minute seemed like an hour as the boy clung desperately to the crack in the mountain. He tried to call out again to Doug, but the words caught in his throat. His fingers began to slip. Bill was filled with panicky fear.

Then there flashed through his mind the memory of his father, whose last words before he died were about the comfort and help to be found in prayer. With this memory, the fear eased and Bill began to pray. The sense of panic left as new strength came to him. He prayed that he could hang on until Doug reached him.

The slow seconds went by. Bill's arms and wrists and fingers were numb with the strain, but now he seemed glued to the ledge. Finally Bill felt someone pushing his feet upward until they were anchored in toeholds. In minutes Doug was pulling him to safety.

The sun was setting as the boys inched themselves to the rocky top. They found a path on the other side leading down off the mountain. Future Justice William O. Douglas of the United States Supreme Court had learned the meaning of prayer.

HIT A HOME RUN FOR ME

Johnny had been in bed all summer with a painful and crippling back ailment. At last the doctors suggested surgery to help him walk, but after the operation Johnny didn't seem to even care about getting well. It was a discouraging time for all who loved the once happy and active boy.

As summer blazed into autumn, he began to think about the World Series, which is played each October to determine the champion baseball team. The year was 1926, and George Herman "Babe" Ruth was the idol of thousands of sports fans all over the world. He was Johnny's special hero.

The day before the Series began, word reached the famous ball player that Johnny lay dying in a New Jersey hospital and that his only interest in life seemed to be baseball.

Early the next morning Babe Ruth was at the hospital. He carried with him a bright new baseball bat, an autographed baseball, and a glove. Sitting at the bedside of the boy, he urged him to fight for life and to grow well and strong so that someday he could play with these gifts.

For the first time in a long while, Johnny smiled;

his pain did not seem half as hard to bear when Babe Ruth held his hand.

"Is there anything else I can do for you, son?" the baseball player asked as he was leaving.

"Yes," said Johnny weakly, "hit a home run for me in the World Series."

"Okay, kid," said Mr. Ruth. "I'll do that—if you promise me you'll get well. Is it a bargain?"

The sick boy nodded in agreement.

That afternoon in Yankee Stadium, Babe Ruth hit a home run. He kept his promise—and so did Johnny Sylvester.

.400 HITTER

Each April when major league baseball begins, people start talking about their favorite teams. They tell of exciting games and great players of the past.

One player they especially remember is Ted Williams, who became a member of the Four Hundred Club, consisting of players who had ended the season with batting averages of .400 or over. Only eight men in all the previous forty years of major league baseball had batted well enough to be honored by membership in this club.

At the beginning of the final week of the season of 1941, Ted's batting average was over .400. His manager asked if Ted would like to be excused from playing ball that week so he wouldn't run a chance of losing this average.

"If I'm going to be a .400 hitter," he said, "I'm going to earn the honor fair and square."

Ted's batting average went down a little that last week of the season. Then came the final afternoon of play. Ted's average stood at .39955—not quite .400, but near enough to be counted as such. Sports writers, baseball fans, and even the manager of the team advised Ted that he should not play that afternoon.

They did not want Ted to take a chance of missing out on becoming the ninth member of the club.

"If I'm going to be a .400 hitter, I want to have more than my toenails on the line," said Ted.

The baseball park in Philadelphia was jammed that afternoon. Each time Ted Williams came to bat, the huge crowd sat in tense silence, almost afraid to breathe for fear of upsetting him. At each hit he made, the crowd roared its approval. The noise almost rocked Philadelphia when the final out was made and the batting average of Ted Williams was a well-earned .406!

A BEACH BASEBALL GAME

The rain had finally stopped. Jeff and John, who had been restlessly watching it all day from their hotel window, were anxious to go outside and continue the vacation the storm had interrupted.

Dad borrowed a bat and ball from the hotel locker room, and the three set out for the beach. They were soon joined by four other boys who had also been hotelbound all day waiting for the storm to pass.

"It's my turn to bat first," called John, and five other boys joined in a chorus: "I'm next; I'm next! I want to hit too!"

Dad pitched the ball to the boys in turn. He was soon soaking wet from scooping their balls out of the surf and thoroughly tired from trying to keep six boys busy and happy. He was ready to call off the game, but eight-year-old Jeff begged him to stay just long enough so each boy could have one more turn at bat.

Jeff's swing connected with the ball, and Dad— tired from the unusual activity—missed the best hit of the afternoon.

Just at that moment a tall, husky, good-looking man who had been watching them play reached out to make a sensational one-handed catch of the ball. The boys let out a spontaneous cheer of approval.

The man tossed the ball to the boys and walked over to Dad. "Mind if I relieve you?" he asked. "A little workout would be good for me, and you look as if you need a rest."

Dad nodded in agreement and sat down to watch. The stranger was soon the center of an admiring group as he patiently coached the boys on how to throw and catch the ball and how to hold the bat.

As the late afternoon deepened into dusk, the man said good-bye. He left without giving his name, but he promised he'd see everyone again soon.

Early the next morning the sun came out in shining splendor. But it did not seem nearly as bright as the smiles on the faces of the half-dozen little boys clustered around the stranger who had played ball with them the previous afternoon.

An older boy on the beach recognized the man, who was busily writing something in Jeff's autograph book. Sprawled across the pages of the book, the boys read as he wrote: "To Jeff, with the best wishes of Stan Musial."

The signature of "Stan-the-Man," one of the all-time greats in baseball, is still treasured. But six boys remember him best for the afternoon he played ball with them on a windy, storm-swept Florida beach.

MARY HAD A LITTLE LAMB

When Tom was a little boy, he wondered about everything. He tried so many experiments and asked so many questions that people laughed at him and called him a dreamer.

When he told them that someday he would make a machine that could talk, they spoke of him as "addlepated." But Tom didn't care. He just went right on wondering and experimenting.

After he became a world-famous inventor, Tom still remembered his boyhood dream of a talking machine. One day he gave one of his helpers a carefully worked out design and told him to build a machine exactly as sketched. When it was finished, Tom wrapped a piece of shiny tinfoil around a cylinder on the little machine and announced it was ready to talk.

The men in the shop bet that the machine wouldn't work. "I'll bet you a barrel of apples that it will," replied Tom as he began to turn a crank attached to the cylinder. He bent over the machine and shouted, "Mary had a little lamb."

The men laughed at the picture Tom made, as well as at the idea that the words he was shouting could be repeated by the strange contraption. The great inventor only smiled as he straightened up, moved the cylinder back to the starting point, and began to turn the crank. Clearly from the machine came back the words, "Mary had a little lamb."

The phonograph had been invented by Thomas Alva Edison. His numerous inventions have brought many shining moments to people all over the world.

THE TYROLESE SONG

The church organ was broken! Christmas was only a few days away, and everyone wondered what would take the place of the organ so there would be music for the Christmas Eve service.

The little Austrian village of Oberndorf lay deep in snow. The winter stars shone brightly through the cold clear night as Father Joseph Mohr plowed through the forest to visit a woodchopper's wife who had given birth to a child.

It was late when he reached the home. In the light of the fire he saw the new mother bending over her tiny infant. They reminded the young priest of Mary and her Baby born in a stable in Bethlehem.

Walking back to the village through the quiet white wintry beauty of the forest, words began to sing together in Father Mohr's head: "Silent night, holy night . . . " Even after he arrived home, the words continued to flow through his mind. It was almost daybreak before he had put them all together, written them down, and gone to bed.

Early the next morning he decided that the words should be put to music. His best friend was Franz Gruber, who taught school and played the church organ, and so he hurried to the Gruber home with his poem. Franz wrote a melody to his friend's words to be sung by two voices accompanied by a guitar.

At the church service in snowy Oberndorf that Christmas Eve of 1818, Franz played the guitar, and he and Father Mohr sang for the first time "Silent Night," the Christmas carol that is loved by children everywhere.

First known as "The Tyrolese Song," it was introduced to the world by four children—two sisters and two brothers—who went to Leipzig one year and sang it so beautifully that the music director of the Kingdom of Saxony asked them to sing the carol at a concert.

In 1850 the Imperial Church choir of Berlin sang the song for King Frederick William IV, who was so delighted that he asked to meet the writer and composer. By that time Father Mohr had died, but Franz Gruber was honored for his music. His guitar is now in the municipal museum at Hallbein.

Each Christmas in remembrance of the Babe of Bethlehem children everywhere sing the lovely "Silent Night" that two friends of Oberndorf, Austria, gave to the world.

BORN TO THE WORK

It was a cold wintry Sunday morning December 9, 1849. As thirty boys and girls stamped in from outdoors, they brushed the snow from their coats and hats and slapped their mittened hands together for warmth.

The children had been invited to come to the home of Richard Ballantyne to begin the first Sunday School ever held in the Salt Lake Valley. As he was building the adobe home, with its stone foundation and dirt roof, he had dreamed of the day when he could gather the neighborhood children around him to tell them the stories of Jesus.

The warmth from the stone fireplace was no brighter than the glow of welcome on the face and in the voice of Richard as he welcomed the children and asked them to take their places on the simple wooden benches he had made for them. When all were quietly seated, the tall bearded man conducted a song and then dedicated the room for the teaching of children.

Years later one of Richard's daughters told of a dream he had had while still a young man. "He saw a large unfinished building," she reported. "He saw a number of young boys playing in and around it. Then he saw an officer of the law after them, trying to catch them. One of the boys ran to my father. With a pitiful, pleading look on his face, he cried, 'Oh, teach me! Teach me!' This dream made such a strong impression that it seemed to point out my father's special work in life."

Richard Ballantyne was born in Whitridgebog, Scotland, August 26, 1817. His father died when Richard was only eleven years old. The young boy was then apprenticed to a baker to learn a trade to help support the family.

Richard was twenty-five and teaching a Sunday School class in the Presbyterian Church when he first heard two Mormon missionaries in a small town near Edinburgh. He was soon baptized. The next year he immigrated to America, where he met his wife. Together they traveled west to the Salt Lake Valley with the early pioneers.

For a year Sunday School was held every Sabbath morning in the Ballantyne home. From that simple beginning, Sunday Schools were organized in other areas and finally became a part of the general organization of the Church.

As he grew older, Richard often said, "I was early called to this work by the voice of the Spirit, and I have felt many times that I had been ordained to this work before I was born, for even before I joined the Church I was moved upon to work for the young."

Boys and girls all over the world can remember with gratitude a little Scottish boy who was "born to the work."

THE BOULDER

The train threaded its way through the mountains that walled Feather River Canyon, carrying its
load of passengers eastward from San Francisco. Although snow lay deep in some of the high passes, a
bright March sun had caused streams to cascade over
the rocks and a soft green to begin to color the oak
brush and grass.

Some of those on the train pressed their faces
against the windows to see the beauty of the canyon.
Others slept.

A man in one of the cars did neither. His thoughts
were of a talk he had been asked to give the following
week at Primary general conference. He wondered
what he might say to express his love for children.

This man was Elder Marion G. Romney, a member of the Quorum of the Twelve Apostles. He picked
up his Bible and turned in the New Testament to the
tenth chapter of Mark, which tells how the Savior
took the children in his arms, put his hands upon
them, and blessed them.

As Elder Romney read, he leaned forward in front
of the window of the train with the New Testament in
his hands and his elbows on his knees. He read and

reread the words until it seemed as if he could see the Savior with the children in His arms. The picture was so beautiful that Elder Romney closed the book, shut his eyes in prayerful thought, and leaned back as far as he could, pressing his body hard against the back of the seat.

Just then a great boulder crashed down the mountainside and burst through the window of the train where he sat. It grazed his face and bruised his right side but did not seriously hurt him.

A week later as Elder Romney stood in the Salt Lake Tabernacle, he said, "Had I been leaning forward, I am sure I should not have been here today." Everyone knew he had been miraculously saved.

FIRE! FIRE!

"Fire! Fire!"

The warning cry brought fear to the hearts of all those in the little community of Farmington, Utah, for it usually meant complete destruction of whatever was burning. They had no equipment to fight fires although everyone who could would form a line and pass buckets of water from the creek to the burning building.

At the first cry of "Fire," Aurelia, who had just arrived in Farmington, ran toward the house from which smoke was billowing up into the hot August air. It belonged to her special friends with whom she often stayed. She had rented her own home that summer and was living in Salt Lake City, a distance of fifteen miles to the south. But she often went to Farmington to "see after things and put up fruit for the winter."

Aurelia joined in the water line. She thought of her friends' loss before she thought of her own. In the upstairs bedroom where she usually slept, she had left some clothes hanging in the closet. Then with a sick feeling she remembered she had also left on a table close to a window the Primary record books.

These books contained the history of the very first Primary ever organized.

"I mourned exceedingly," said Aurelia later. "I would not have minded losing my clothes (I had a nice plush cape, a dress, and some other things burned) if the records could only have been saved."

Aurelia was heartsick as she returned to Salt Lake after helping her friends move into a nearby vacant house. But the loss of the record books haunted her. In a few days she went back to Farmington to gather information to write another history of the organization of the Primary.

What thrilling news awaited her there! These are her own words telling about it:

Brother Moroni Secrist, who was bishop of our ward at the time, felt prompted to climb onto the porch and go through the window to my room, thinking he might save some of the property, but when he went inside the smoke was so dense he was nearly suffocated and had to be helped out by others who had followed. As he neared the window he reached out his hand and felt the cover on the table and drew it toward him, gathering up the corners with the books and a box of notions that I had, and passed them to those on the outside. Thus the records were saved through the providence of God.

Aurelia Rogers' rescued history of the organization of the first Primary is even more precious today.

THE SURPRISE PARTY

From her porch rocking chair, Aurelia watched the evening sky as the sun set in a flame of scarlet over the Great Salt Lake. Then as the sunset colors faded into grays and blues, a cool breeze blew off the lake.

Aurelia sighed softly as she pulled her paisley shawl tight across her thin shoulders. She had not been feeling well for some time now and knew she should soon go inside, but something about the evening held her on the porch.

Suddenly the evening sounds were lost as strains of music grew loud in the air. Aurelia leaned forward in her chair and looked to the east from where the music came.

Down the dusty road marched the Farmington Silver Band followed by a number of buggies. The procession stopped in front of Aurelia's home. From the buggies jumped a dozen friends who called out warm greetings. They had come, they said, to take Aurelia to the meetinghouse.

Aurelia felt an unusual air of excitement in the little rock chapel. Planks had been laid on sawhorses to make long tables. On each table was a snowy white cloth. The tables were quickly set with steaming pots of stewed chicken, mashed potatoes, and gravy that had been prepared in home kitchens and brought to the meetinghouse.

The building was filled with boys and girls, relatives, and friends—many of whom had traveled for hours to be on hand for the surprise party that had been planned to honor Aurelia.

After dinner there was a program. Talks were given, a history of the Primary was read, and songs especially written for the occasion were sung. The Primary children and many who had been Primary children had made a flower picture within a large frame. When they helped Aurelia to the stand to receive it, every person in the little rock chapel arose to pay tribute to this gentle woman who had been called fourteen years before to preside over a Primary in Farmington, Utah.

Aurelia, with tears glistening in her eyes, put out her arms to all of her "children" as she thanked them. It was a shining moment in the life of Aurelia Spencer Rogers, who conducted the first Primary ever held for boys and girls.

SHINING MOMENTS
IN THE LIVES
OF MISSIONARIES
AND SERVICEMEN

THE LETTER

The prison guard brought a letter to the jail cell. The three young men inside were very surprised, for none of them had received mail or visitors for weeks.

One prisoner had been charged with murder, and another had been arrested as a tramp. The third— and youngest—was an American who had been brought to the prison because he was distributing missionary tracts and telling the people of Austria about Joseph Smith and The Church of Jesus Christ of Latter-day Saints, which he said had been organized under inspiration in America.

Thomas Biesinger was alone the morning two police officers pulled him out of bed. They said that a Protestant minister had signed a complaint against him and that he was under arrest. He was taken to a small dirty jail cell furnished with only three hardstraw mattresses. No food or drink was given to him for more than twenty-four hours, and he wondered if he would ever live to leave the place.

The two prisoners already confined in the cell and many of the guards spoke only in ridicule to the heartsick and homesick young elder. They believed he was a leader from America who had come to Austria to persuade people to become Mormon slaves.

Now the three inmates watched the guard wave the letter in the air. No one moved. Finally the guard motioned for Elder Biesinger to take the envelope.

A letter! What an unexpected break in the long days that had stretched into more than a month of lonely imprisonment.

The letter was about Elder Hammer, his former companion, who had gone to Germany two weeks before Elder Biesinger's arrest. The letter reported that Elder Hammer was critically ill with smallpox and desperately in need of help.

Elder Biesinger begged for permission to visit his friend for just a few days. He promised to return and spend extra time in jail, but permission was denied. Finally the jailer agreed to let Elder Biesinger write a letter to his companion, provided the prisoner would go before the judge and receive approval for the letter to be sent.

All day and all night Elder Biesinger fervently offered silent prayers for his sick companion and for guidance in writing the letter. At last he began to put on paper the thoughts that came to him. He promised in the name of Jesus Christ that through the power of the priesthood Elder Hammer would live and return to his family.

The next morning the young prisoner appeared before the judge. When the judge read and reread the unusual letter, he was silent for a long time. He looked at the young man before him and then reread the letter. Finally the judge finished reading, was silent a moment, and then quietly gave permission for the letter to be sent.

Although there had been little hope for Elder

Hammer's recovery, the promise given in the letter was soon fulfilled!

Some weeks later Elder Biesinger was released from prison, and he began once more to teach the people in Austria who would listen. One person who listened and was later baptized a member of the Church was a police official who had been greatly impressed by the missionary while he was in prison.

Before long another elder was sent from the Swiss and German Mission so Elder Biesinger would again have a companion. Soon after his arrival, though, the two young men were visited by police officers, who gave them only twenty-four hours to pack and leave the country.

After World War I, Elder Biesinger was again called to go back to Austria. This time he stayed long enough to help establish a strong mission in that country.

Today many people in Austria are members of the Church. Church members are viewed with much more favor by the government and other people than they were when Thomas Biesinger wrote his remarkable letter from a dirty little jail cell and blessed a desperately ill elder.

THE GIFT OF FAITH

As the missionaries came to a small fishing shack located off the beaten track in New Zealand, an old Maori man hurried inside to find an envelope in which he had stuffed a sizable sum of hard-earned money. He promptly handed the envelope containing the money to the missionaries.

Inside the envelope was a letter from the mission office addressed to the man. He could not read English, but he could recognize the figures contained in the letter. He thought the mission needed for some special purpose the cash amount mentioned, and he had it all ready.

After the missionaries translated the letter for him, he was surprised to learn that the letter was a receipt for last year's tithing. His faith was so strong that he was willing and ready to pay the same amount over again if the Lord's servants needed it for the work of the gospel.

CHRISTMAS PRAYERS

It was a cold and dreary Christmas Eve for all of England on December 24, 1939—especially for the soldiers in the platoon commanded by David Niven. The famous British actor had arrived from Hollywood only a short time before as a volunteer.

There were forty men in the platoon, and all forty were unhappy about many things. They had not been given liberty to spend Christmas Eve with their families as they had expected, and they were quartered in a shabby stable near Dover. They had no bedding except the straw that was in the stable, and they resented having David Niven as their commander. Their remarks revealed that they felt he could act out bravery in motion pictures but had none of his own.

As David lay on the straw, he wondered if he dared to kneel and say his prayers as he had done every night of his life. Here in this stable on Christmas Eve seemed an especially right time to say a prayer, yet he was afraid all forty of those tough soldiers would think he was just putting on an act.

Finally, however, he gathered his courage and knelt down. His prayer was one of gratitude for loved ones far away and for the Christ child born so long ago in a stable. The loud laughter, the sarcastic remarks, and then even the quieter snickers stopped.

As David Niven finished his prayer, he looked around him. There in the shabby little stable at least a dozen of England's roughest soldiers knelt in the straw to say their Christmas Eve prayers while the others watched in silent wonderment.

A MISSION TO THE LAMANITES

"The seed of Manasseh," Melvin repeated to himself just as he had more than forty years before when, as a boy of eleven, he had first heard these words.

It had been at the time the Logan Temple was dedicated and Patriarch Zebedee Coltrin had traveled from his home in southern Utah to stay with Melvin's family and attend the dedication. What a thrill it was for Melvin to meet a man who had personally known the Prophet Joseph Smith!

Every morning Melvin arose early so he could shine the patriarch's shoes and listen to more stories about the Prophet.

Before leaving for home, Brother Coltrin suggested that he give a special blessing to Melvin and some of his brothers and sisters. In Melvin's blessing the patriarch declared, "Thou shalt proclaim the gospel unto the seed of Manasseh and shall do many mighty miracles in the midst of the Lord."

Later Melvin's father told the family the story of Ephraim and Manasseh. Then he read to them from the Book of Mormon about Lehi and his family, who were descendants of Manasseh. He explained that the Indians were Lamanites and were known as the seed of Manasseh.

During the following years Melvin thought many times about his blessing. The only Lamanites he had ever seen were those who lived in tents outside of the little pioneer town of Logan, and he often wondered how he could proclaim the gospel to them.

Now, more than forty years later, Melvin J. Ballard was aboard a ship sailing for Buenos Aires, where he and his two companions, Elders Rulon G. Wells and Rey L. Pratt, were to open a mission for the South American people. As he walked along the windswept deck of the steamship *Voltaire,* he thought he finally understood the words of the inspired patriarch many years before. He felt that the promise of his blessing was about to be fulfilled.

The steamship docked at Buenos Aires early on the morning of December 6, 1925, and that very afternoon the three elders met with twelve adults and four children who were interested in learning more about the restored gospel of Jesus Christ.

Melvin recorded in his diary December 12: "Just as the sun was going down, I baptized six people in the Rio de la Plata, the first in this generation in South America." The next day the six were confirmed in a meeting, and the sacrament was administered to them for the first time.

Christmas night of that same year Melvin again wrote in his diary: "The sun came up at 4:51. We were up at 5. We arrived at Park 3 de Febrero at a place near the river in a grove of weeping willows at 7 A.M. We sang 'The Morning Breaks.' Brother Pratt read several passages from the Book of Mormon on promises of redemption of the Lamanites. Brother Wells read from the Bible. We all knelt under a weeping willow tree, and I offered prayer."

Here is part of the prayer Elder Ballard offered: "We are grateful to come to this great land of South America to unlock the door for the preaching of the gospel. We thank thee for the few who have received us and for those we have had the joy of taking into the waters of baptism in this land. May they be the first fruits of a glorious harvest."

As Melvin J. Ballard left Buenos Aires, Argentina, July 4, 1926, he reported to the members of the Church who had gathered to say good-bye that "the work of the Lord will grow slowly for a time. It will not shoot up in a day as does the sunflower that grows quickly and then dies. But thousands will join the Church here."

This promise has been fulfilled many times over in Argentina and other South American "Book of Mormon" countries. The seed of Manasseh comprises a great part of the Church in that land as well as in other parts of the world.

THE STAR-SPANGLED BANNER

One summer day prisoners of war in a foreign prison camp had just completed a talent show. Without any announcement two soldiers holding a rolled-up blanket suddenly stood up in front of the group. They looked quickly but carefully to see that no guards were watching. Then, holding the blanket high, they let it unroll. There, fastened to the inside of the blanket was their country's flag!

At the time of surrender one of the soldiers had taken down the flag and wrapped it around his body. Then he had put on his uniform so the flag might not be discovered during the inspection of his belongings. He had hidden it until he got to the prison camp.

When the men saw the flag that the blanket had concealed, a ripple of wonder and amazement spread throughout the group. This was followed almost instantly by the deep silence that comes only when one's heart is too full to permit words to be spoken.

With their eyes still gazing upon the colorful banner, the soldiers began to sing. Softly but with increasing depth of feeling, the boys sang their national anthem.

A HEAVENLY MISSION

Many great and spiritual experiences have taken place in the Alberta Temple. Among them was one that resulted from the fervent prayers of the parents of a young elder who drowned while on his way to a mission in South America. His grieving father and mother could not be comforted.

One evening while the father was in the Alberta Temple, he heard his son's voice, although he did not see him. The young elder told his father that the grieving of his parents was making it impossible for him to fill the heavenly mission to which he had been called. Then the boy promised that as a witness to the importance of the work he had been called to do, the father would be asked to speak at a special meeting that day in the temple.

Unexpectedly that afternoon the temple president stopped the work of those in the temple and announced that there would be a testimony meeting. He asked several people to participate, and the father anxiously awaited his time. When another man was announced as the concluding speaker, the sorrowing father left the meeting fearful that the visit with his son had been only his imagination.

Before the man left the building, however, the temple president arose and announced that he had heard a voice directing him to ask this man to speak to the group. Those in the room reported that the father had left. "Then go and find him," the president urged.

When the father returned to the meeting, he told the group of his unusual experience, while tears of comfort and joy glistened in his peace-filled eyes.

IS IT REALLY TRUE?

Sam John could hardly wait until class was over so he could talk with Brother Murphy. He had an important question to ask—one that he didn't want anyone else to hear.

At first Sam had gone to Brother Murphy's classes because he liked being with the older boys and girls who attended. Then he kept going because of the lovely music. Finally he realized that what he enjoyed more than anything else was the feeling he had when he listened to Brother Murphy's teachings.

Now Sam John had to know if what Brother Murphy was teaching were really true. So he waited patiently until almost everyone had left the class. Then he went up to the white-haired man to ask if he could talk with him alone.

A bench under a spreading tree made a perfect place for Sam to ask the teacher his important question. "Brother Murphy," he began, "are these things you have told us about Jesus and Joseph Smith really true?"

The man looked down, surprised that a boy only eight years old could be so serious and sincere. Then he took the boy's hand, looked into his eyes, and asked a question too. "Sam," he said, "do you think Sister Murphy and I and all the other missionaries who have been teaching these classes would spend money to come to Hawaii and take our precious time to tell you these things if we did not know they are true?"

Without hesitation, Sam answered, "I believe these things too, and I want to be baptized into your church."

Then Sam told Brother Murphy that his mother had been baptized when she was just a little girl, but she didn't understand much about the Church and had never been active in it.

"What would she think if you were baptized?" Brother Murphy asked Sam. "And what about your father?"

Sam had to admit that he didn't think his father would be very happy with his son's interest in the Church, but he promised to talk to him.

A few days later Sam John's father, a Chinese-Hawaiian, went to the mission home. "What is this you have been teaching my son?" he demanded. "He even wants to become a member of your church."

"Mr. John," President Murphy answered. "I'm glad you've come to talk with me. There is nothing we have taught Sam that you should not also know, especially since your boy wants to be baptized."

The next night Sam's father returned to the mission home to be taught—and the next and the next. Sam could hardly believe it when a few weeks later his father suggested that Sam wait to be baptized so that he and Sam's older brother could be baptized too.

"Now we are united as a family," Sam thought after he and his father and brother were baptized. And it seemed as if he would burst with happiness.

WE WERE THERE

It was just before dawn. Slowly the anxious moments ticked by for the American soldiers, who waited in boats for the signal that would start their battle. They were trying to take a Japanese island base in the Pacific during World War II.

At twenty minutes to six, the signal came to start firing. Suddenly it was as though the island base and all the boats waiting to attack exploded into flame and fire. Dive bombers dropped their loads, machine guns cut down the men who had started wading toward shore, and the island base of Kwajalein seemed to heave and roll with the fury of the battle.

In one of the boats were two young Latter-day Saint marines. These two marines were hit in the first wave of gunfire, and one was very badly wounded. The other, who was less seriously hurt, held the head of his comrade above water until help came. Finally, a United Press newspaperman and some medics found them both in the water. They tried to give first aid to the least injured boy, but he refused help until his buddy was checked.

The rescuers thought the marine was too badly

hurt to ever recover. A war correspondent wrote the rest of the story February 8, 1944:

> Then it happened. This young man, the stronger of the two, bronzed by the tropical sun, clean as a shark's tooth in the South Seas, slowly got to his knees. His own arm was nearly gone, but with the other he lifted the head of his unconscious pal into his lap, placed his good hand on the other's pale brow, and uttered what to us seemed to be incredible words—words that to this moment are emblazoned in unforgettable letters across the doorway of my memory: "In the name of Jesus Christ, and by virtue of the holy priesthood which I hold, I command you to remain alive until the necessary help can be obtained to secure the preservation of your life."

The two young marines were later taken to a hospital with the newspaper reporter, who concluded:

> The three of us are here in Honolulu, and today we walked down the beach together. . . . He is the wonder of the medical unit, for—they say—he should be dead. Why he isn't they don't know—but we do—for we were there, off the shores of Kwajalein.

THE STRANGE CHECK

The little boat making its way slowly from England to South Africa had been tossed by storms for more than six weeks. Aboard was Elder Franklin D. Price, a young Mormon missionary.

Each day Elder Price became more worried, for food and money were scarce. According to the law of the Union of South Africa, no one was permitted to enter that country unless he had at least twenty dollars with him. Elder Price did not have the required sum.

When the boat finally docked, the young elder decided that he would board a train and go as far as he possibly could. As he walked off the ship, he noticed a small folded piece of paper lying at the foot of the gangplank. Without thinking, he stooped down, picked it up, and automatically slipped the paper into his pocket.

In no time he was on a train speeding down the tracks toward the Union of South Africa. At the border, immigration officials came aboard to check all entry papers. Elder Price was worried about what would happen to him when the officials discovered that he had no money.

When the men approached, Elder Price felt a moment of panic. Then, without even knowing why, he reached into his pocket and pulled out the piece of paper he had found earlier. Elder Price handed the paper to one of the officials. The man nodded his head and returned the paper to the astonished young elder. That paper was an endorsed check in the amount of twenty dollars with the stamp of the Union of South Africa affixed.

THE ANSWER

The boys and girls in the third grade were expecting a letter. Every day they eagerly waited for the mail to be distributed. The letters to which they so much wanted an answer had been written months before in 1943. Now it was March 1944.

World War II was being fought on battlefields far away, and several of the children's fathers and brothers were members of the armed forces. All the class wanted to help so these fathers and brothers could be home with their families.

The children had talked about what to do but could not decide what would be best, so each had written a letter to the commanding general.

One letter had explained, "Bill, my big brother, he got killed. . . . I want to help win the war 'cause Bill'd want me to help."

Phil, whose father was a prisoner of war, had written simply, "Please, if there is one thing I can do, you'll tell me."

Another letter had begun, "Please to tell us how to help you win this war. My daddy is over there with you. . . . I want to help so he can come home."

No answer had come to the letters. The children's

teacher had almost given up hope there would ever be one, but she did not voice her discouragement. She felt sure that if an answer came at all, it would be from the general's secretary and would merely acknowledge the letters. She wondered what she could say then to the disappointed children.

The long minutes ticked slowly away. It was past time for the mail to be delivered. Another school day was almost over and still no letter. The teacher sighed, and the boys and girls echoed her sigh.

Just then a man stopped in the open doorway. Every eye in the class was instantly focused on the letter in his hand. A breathless hush came over the third grade as the teacher started toward the door. Then the children surged ahead of her, took the letter, gave it to her, and stood close as she began to read aloud:

Dear Boys and Girls:
. . . I have been so long in answering. . . . Your messages did not reach me until today because they had to follow me a long way. . . .

The letter suggested that the children should give their Pledge to the Flag at least once a week, offer prayers, support the Red Cross, write to their fathers and brothers, and learn all they could about their country and be grateful for it. The general promised that if they did all these things, they could feel that they had served their country as if they were soldiers themselves.

The letter was signed, "Sincerely, General Dwight D. Eisenhower."

There was a moment of silence, and then one child cried, "He did answer! He told us how to help!"

NO PLACE TO STAY

Two young elders were beginning to feel desperate for a place to stay. They had knocked at many doors in the little English village and they had talked with members of the Church and nonmembers. No one was interested in giving "digs" (a room with meals provided) to two Mormon missionaries.

The elders felt that they had checked every possibility and that they had wasted days in following leads. But their efforts had met with failure after failure. They had prayed for help but no help had come.

Then the elders decided that there was just one last thing to do—add fasting to their prayers. One of them was so discouraged that he was doubtful whether even this would bring results, but he was willing to try anything.

Whenever the missionaries had a problem, they usually fasted for only twenty-four hours, but when these two young men had not found a place to live after that period of time, they decided to fast for another day and night. After forty-eight hours of fasting and prayer, the young men still had not been successful. By this time they had returned to the same tracting area for the second time.

Hardly knowing whether they were being guided by inspiration or desperation, one of them was impressed to knock on a door from which they had been rather rudely turned away the first time they had called. There was no answer, but a neighbor saw the elders and recognized them. She remembered their request and called out, "You're still looking for a place to live, aren't you?"

When they told her they were, she said, "Well, I happen to know a lady who is looking for some people to live with her." As it turned out, this was a perfect place for the elders to stay.

Said one of the elders in telling the experience later: "We gratefully recognized that the Lord had accepted our fast and answered our prayers. I gained more of an understanding of my Heavenly Father. We should have fasted at first, for He directed us only after we started fasting and had put forth considerable effort and after there was sufficient sacrifice."

A SPECIAL PARTY FOR DAD

"I just know it's going to be the best party in the whole world," one of the girls remarked, and the others nodded in agreement.

"But it won't be the best party for me," thought ten-year-old Kim, "if Dad doesn't get home from Vietnam until the end of January."

As the girls went on talking excitedly about the daddy-daughter party scheduled for the following Friday, Kim was thinking how wonderful it would be if only her father could be at home every night just as he used to be. That was before he left his family for overseas duty, where he was busy flying his helicopter *Hereafter 727* in the area around Saigon.

That evening after the four younger children were asleep, Kim went to her mother's room and tried to explain how important it was for Dad to come home in time to go to the party the girls in her Primary class were planning.

"I know how much you want him home," Mother said soothingly, "and I know too that he is anxious to be here with you. But you must understand that it is an absolute impossibility for Daddy to be home by next Friday night. He would be if he could, but he won't be given leave for at least three more weeks."

Kim listened quietly, but as she kissed her mother goodnight she said, "I won't stop hoping that Daddy will be able to come home ahead of schedule. In fact, I'm going to pray that he will. If I ask Heavenly Father to please let Daddy come home in time for the party, he just might be here."

Kim didn't see Mother shake her head, nor did she know how anxiously Mother watched her little girl go thoughtfully off to bed.

Early next Sunday morning as Kim and her brothers and sisters were getting ready for Sunday School, they thought they heard someone in the kitchen. When Mother made a funny choking noise, they ran to see what was happening. With gasps of surprise and joy, they welcomed their father, who tried to hug them all at once and then each one in turn.

"I don't know how it happened," he told them, "but last Thursday my commanding officer just walked in and said to me, 'You'll soon be going home anyhow, so why don't you go right now!' It didn't take me long to pack my duds, and here I am! Let's all go to church together!"

The daddy-daughter party the following Friday was a special event for each girl who attended with her dad, but the happiest one of all was Kim as she walked in through the doorway on the arm of her proud father.

PAYING A DEBT

One night in 1970 fifteen-year-old Dan Ecklund rang the doorbell of the mission home in Zurich, Switzerland. When President M. Elmer Christensen opened the door, Dan said he wanted to talk with someone who could tell him about The Church of Jesus Christ of Latter-day Saints.

Dan and his family had been living in the Congo and were on their way back to the United States. For eighteen years his father and mother had been serving as Protestant missionaries in the Congo, where all seven of their children had been born. They had not been happy when Dan became interested in another church while on vacation in South Africa and asked their permission to be baptized. However, Dan was so convinced that the new church was true that finally his parents consented to let Dan be baptized.

Since the mission president in Zurich had supervision over any members in the Congo, Dan had written to ask President Christensen to send him some books to study. He had persuaded his father to let the family stop in Zurich on their way to the United

States so he could ask President Christensen to explain some things he did not understand.

While the rest of the Ecklund family visited with Sister Christensen, Dan went into President Christensen's office, where they sat down and quietly discussed some of his questions.

Before Dan stood up to leave, he opened his wallet and took out a five-dollar bill in American money. He said that since he had become a member of the Church, he had earned forty-five dollars. This meant he owed four dollars and fifty cents tithing. The boy wanted to make a fifty-cent donation with the balance of the bill.

President Christensen explained about fast offerings, and Dan quickly agreed that this was a good place for his fifty cents to go. So the mission president wrote out a receipt and handed it to the boy, who read it thoughtfully and then tucked it into his wallet.

With a huge smile, he left the mission office and joined the rest of his family. Dan felt that at last he was truly a member of the Church he had learned to love.

SPECIAL BLESSINGS

Twenty people crowded into the small home of
Erich Konietz in Selbongen, Poland. Some had
traveled more than nine hours to get to Selbongen,
and among them were seven young children. These
boys and girls weren't old enough to understand just
what the meeting meant, but they could feel the wonder and excitement of friends being together again.

The date was October 17, 1970. Percy Fetzer of
Salt Lake City, Utah, had been specially ordained by
the First Presidency of the Church to give patriarchal blessings to members of the Church behind the
Iron Curtain. M. Elmer Christensen, president of the
Switzerland Mission, had arranged for him to go to
Selbongen and had sent word to the members of the
branch to meet with him on that wonderful Saturday
afternoon.

President Christensen first told the group about
the death of David O. McKay, the ninth president of
the Church. He had been able to bring a picture of
Joseph Fielding Smith, who was the new tenth president. He told the group the names of all of the General Authorities and had them say the names again

and again until even the young children could repeat them.

Sister Fetzer and Sister Christensen told the Saints about Sunday School and Primary programs for children. Young and old learned some songs, including "I Am a Child of God," which they especially liked. No one there had heard this song before, and they learned the words quickly and sang it with great feeling. Although they couldn't write the words down on paper, they recorded the melody in their hearts and minds.

The members of the Selbongen Branch who crowded into the Konietz home had once been free to enjoy each other and their membership in the Church. They had even built a small chapel in 1928—the first chapel of the Church ever built in Germany. But in 1945 war came to their country, and many of them left their homes to escape the invading Russian army.

Some of the Church members who fled walked for days, taking with them only what they could carry. Others loaded their belongings into handcarts. A few were able to scramble aboard trains. Many died trying to escape.

Those who stayed in their own homes and survived the horrors of war found afterward that they were no longer citizens of Germany. Their land had been given to Poland. Because of this the people had to endure many hardships, and they were greatly limited in where they could go and what they could do.

In spite of these difficulties, however, the small group of Church members managed to meet together. They were more than six hundred miles from any other Latter-day Saints, but by a miracle their lives and their chapel had been spared. Their hearts were full of gratitude.

Now they were meeting together, hearing news of their brothers and sisters and receiving patriarchal blessings from Brother Fetzer. It was a wonderful day!

While giving the blessings, Brother Fetzer was inspired to promise some that if they lived the gospel they would go to a temple. He promised others that they would go on missions. These things seemed impossible on that day in October 1970, but since that time a temple has been dedicated in East Germany and many German people living in Poland have been able to move to West Germany. All of the promised blessings for the Saints of Selbongen will someday be fulfilled.

THE KITCHEN VISIT

Everyone was excited. Tonight a special cere-mony would honor the twelve-year-old girls who would soon become members of the church that had established the school. The girls had washed and ironed their white dresses and gathered flowers to decorate the chapel.

Those who had been selected to help with refresh-ments were in the kitchen. It was a hot humid day, not unlike many in Samoa, but the girls didn't seem to mind either the work or the heat as they laughed together.

Only Foi was quiet and uneasy. She tried again to remember what she could of the years before she had been sent to the school for medical care and to learn to read. At night when the girls in her room were asleep, Foi often tried to put together fragments of her memories and assure herself that someday her family would send for her. Foi knew this would be hard to do, for they lived in a faraway Samoan village that few people ever left and where strangers seldom went.

Foi remembered that once two young men had come to her home. They said they were missionaries, and they had taught those of her village. Even though she had been only a little girl, Foi remembered the good feeling that had come to her as she listened to these missionaries and heard about their church. She longed to have that feeling again. But severe storms had come soon after their visit, and the missionaries had not returned before Foi had been sent to the school.

"Maybe it is the memory of the missionaries that makes me unsure about the church of the school," Foi reasoned. She wished with all the fervor of her twelve years that she could see the young men again before joining this other church.

For months Foi had prayed that she would know what was the right decision for her to make before the night came for the membership meeting. She had tried to tell her teachers she was not ready to become a member of their church, but they had only laughed at her. "You are already past twelve," they said. "You will never see your village again. It is time you became one of us."

The girls finished their work in the kitchen and left. Only Foi lingered. She bowed her head and murmured a fervent prayer that she might know what was the right thing for her to do.

When she raised her head, she saw two young men at the door.

"We are looking for Foi Frost," they said. "We are Mormon missionaries. Her family has joined our church and have sent us to take her back to her village."

Foi smiled as her eyes filled with tears. Her prayers had been answered. Not only would she see her family again, but she would be able to learn about the church that her heart told her was true.

TOPICAL INDEX